EAT THE BURRITO

It Could Save Your Life

Joni Davis

Christy~
In this crazy world you have been a refreshing & caring voice.
All my love.
Joni!

To my husband, Craig, who never left my side.

Introduction

I have had the opportunity to consult in many different industries and for many notable organizations, including: NASCAR, large vacation resorts, a national jewelry chain and several amusement parks; but my one true passion has always been working in the automotive industry. Throughout my 30 years (*and counting*) in the automotive industry, I have seen it all. I have organized every type of customer event for my clients, including: promotional events at movie theatres, amusement parks, and malls. Through my efforts, I have proudly helped my clients grow more than 100% by being strong, inventive and *oh* so human- as you will soon learn.

There is no question that my experiences on the road were entertaining. If we had all the time in the world, I could tell you thousands of stories about my visits to dealerships across the world and all the characters I met along the way, but alas, life is short, and so I have tucked 15 of my favorite stories between each chapter of my life story.

It is my hope that once you have finished reading *Eat the Burrito*, you will remember the events of my life and remember the one rule I always choose to follow:

Never lose your sense of humor *or* your self-respect.

Chapter 1 | Where It All Began

I was born in Madison, Wisconsin on a cold, snowy day in February of 1959. Looking back on it, I always felt as though I was meant to be a child of the '60s, but unfortunately, my parents just could not wait that one measly extra year. Born the youngest of three sisters, however, I was blissfully content being the center of attention in my family.

My mother was a stay-at-home mom for most of my life, so my sisters and I had a habitual daily routine. Each morning we woke up and raced to the kitchen where we battled each other for our beloved cereal of choice- mine was frosted flakes, theirs were Cheerios and Rice Krispies. After breakfast, if the temperamental Midwest weather allowed, we gathered with our neighborhood friends for endless games of tag and hide-and-seek. For the inevitable (and frequent) times our childhood antics got on my mother's nerves, she would always turn to us and warn, "Just wait until your father comes home." And sure enough, every day at 5:00 PM, like clockwork, my father would walk through our front door.

My father was an intimidating figure to me. It was clear that he was the "captain" of our ship and a force to be reckoned with. My father was a classic disciplinarian that demanded order- especially around the dinner table- so everybody, including our dog, an adorable mutt named Heinz, would always be on their best behavior.

Heinz joined the family before I was old enough to know what a dog was. He was sweet, playful and stuck to us like a shadow. Funny enough, as many dogs do, Heinz absolutely could not stand our mailman. Day after day, Heinz would always bark at the kind mail carrier, who always chuckled at the persistence of our dog. It was all fun and games, until we realized one day that the gate had been left open. Heinz ran right after the poor mailman and proceeded to bite him. Usually everyone's mind wanders to a vicious animal attack, but to be clear, it was only one little bite. Poor Heinz was definitely in the "dog house" now. Once my father returned home that evening, I overheard our parents talking about solutions. The next day, Heinz was brought to a nearby farm. I missed him so very much and always dreamed that he was happier there with more space to run, and other animals to chase.

-

A few years later, my father told me the story of what happened to Heinz while living at the farm. One day the farmer found himself inside a pen with an angry bull. As this big, ferocious animal began to take charge towards the farmer, Heinz jumped into the pen and distracted the bull. Through his act of heroism, the farmer was able to escape the pen unharmed. Unfortunately, Heinz was not so lucky. Although my father's story did not have a happy ending, I smiled knowing that Heinz died a hero.

-

That summer we gave ol' Heinz away, my parents gave us the big news that we would be adding a new family member. Yes, my mom was pregnant. The news gave my five-year-old self a great deal of mixed feelings. As mentioned earlier, I quite enjoyed being the youngest child. But now, in the blink of an eye, I suddenly became a middle child, desperately searching for the attention I once knew all too well.

My baby sister, Jane, was born in May, and even though I hated to admit it, she was beautiful. The first few months of big-sisterhood went by rather smoothly, until my first day of school that fall. It was my first day of kindergarten, and I really hated the idea of leaving home. My mother placed Jane in the stroller, and they walked me to school. I reluctantly entered the massive building and then turned right back around. I believe I had a "little person's panic attack". Perhaps it was the thought of all that extra attention and one on one time my sister would be receiving was too overwhelming to me. As I walked up the front steps and rang the doorbell, I could see my mom and my sister in the window. Tears ran down my cheeks as I realized that my mother was going to choose to ignore me standing there. I stood on that front porch for several hours. In fact, it wasn't until my older sisters came home that I was let back inside.

It simply felt like the most hurtful gesture.

From that day forward, I often doubted a part of my own sense of self-worth, wondering if I was "enough." What was missing in me that urged my mom to ignore my feelings? Reflecting on that now, these moments drastically shaped the role I would later play as a mother. I internally vowed that I would never undervalue any of my children's feelings or worth.

Stories from the Road: Number 1

NEVER TAKE NO

I began my consulting career in the automotive industry by selling training to dealership owners- commonly referred to as car dealers. The training I sold was designed to help sales people improve their communication with customers and sell more cars- skills every dealer longed for their sales people to have.

As with any sales job, the word "No" was thrown at me daily. However, early in my career of selling training to car dealers, I learned a technique that resulted in the best close rate I had ever seen. It worked like this:

After my presentation, if a dealer told me they weren't interested in buying my training, I would pick up my briefcase and casually ask who their direct competitor was.

"Why do you want to know that?" They always asked quizzically.

"Because that's my next stop," I would respond, guiding them gently to my foolproof close.

"Well, I don't want them to have this training..."

Sitting back down in the chair, I would pull out the contract again and say, "Then just sign here."

SOLD!

Chapter 2 | The Love Story

My mom grew up in a large family, with parents that loved each other unconditionally. Her father was a fireman and her mother stayed at home with her and her four younger siblings. Their house, I was told, was constantly filled with visiting relatives. This made for a robust and delightfully strong sense of family.

My mother loved to dance. She took lessons for her entire life, and when she could not afford them at times, she found a way to assist with providing skill training to younger kids to get her own lessons for free. I always found it strange that, with four daughters of her own, she did not put any of us into dance. It was as if she needed to keep it for herself.

As the oldest of five children, my mother was thrust into a leadership role at a young age. It was common practice for her parents to safety pin the gas bill payment to her coat and send her on a bus to go pay it. I always visualized this seven-year-old sitting proudly on the bus, alone, en route to make utility payments. Yes, it was a very different time.

Taking care of her siblings was a natural part of my mother's upbringing. Perhaps it was her innate ability to care for others that made her such a good match for my dad. He deeply needed to be cared for, and she knew exactly how to provide that- even if it meant frequently putting herself second.

Unlike my mother, my father was an only child, and, by his descriptions, a very lonely one. His parents married in their 20s and were determined to leave the farms they grew up on. They made their way to the big city of Madison with hopes to escape the never-ending tedium of farm life. In the end, though, it seemed they traded one sort of never-ending work for another. They opened a tavern with a restaurant and convenience store in Westport, Wisconsin, and lived above their place of work.

My dad grew up very involved with the family business, serving drinks to the bar patrons at 5 and rolling cigarettes by 10. At the age of 13, he lied about his age and got a job driving a truck for a local canning company. His legs weren't long enough to reach the truck pedals, so he tied a brick on his right foot. In high school, my father sold cigarettes to his peers outside of sporting events. It was in these stories I gained a sense of my father's innate drive and work ethic, while realizing I possess many of the same traits.

Now, growing up under such responsibility-bearing circumstances clearly took a toll on my father. I believe he did not get to experience the true value of family- at least, not the way little boys imagine. He wanted a normal work routine, Monday thru Friday, and a wife with children to come home to. He saw these lives all around him in the patrons that frequented his parents' business, but not in his own life. His idea of family was shaped by his German-raised parents, who placed emphasis on discipline and chores over affection. That lack of affection resulted in a tough outer shell, a guard that was difficult to break through. With my father, it was as if letting kindness in would make him weak.

With a signed permission slip from his parents, my Dad enlisted in the Navy as soon as he graduated from high school at the age of 17. He did this, I believe, not out of patriotism, but because he was a young man in search of camaraderie and an escape from his isolated home life. My father became a corpsman, and although was away from home, he grew by taking his first adult steps on his own.

In early November 1953, fate would place my parents at the same wedding dance in Waunakee, Wisconsin. My mother's eyes fell upon a handsome man, while my father had already thought of the perfect pick-up line. "Did you come here to get warm, or do you want to dance?"

"I came to dance", she replied. (You are probably wondering how I can quote those lines, but it is a fact that I have heard this story from my mother no less than 200 times over the span of my life.)

My dad was not only a handsome man, but a good dancer. A quality my mother valued greatly, given her love for dance. He stole her heart that night, and she stole his. They danced until the lights came on and he asked if he could drive her home. She, of course, said yes, however he had to agree to take her friends home, too. After this night ended, my parents would go on to see each other every night until he had to return to his base in Bremerton, Washington.

They went approximately two miserable weeks without each other, when my father offered a strong ultimatum, "Come out to Bremerton and marry me, or I will go AWOL."

He bought her a one-way ticket, and my Mom left her home on December 24th, leaving her family and the home she knew to marry a virtual stranger. They were wed on December 26th and would stay happily married for over 55 years.

It is a rarity to find such fast and true love, or perhaps it was the stars aligning. They always hoped that my sisters and I would find this same love, but a love like that is not easy to find.

Stories from the Road: Number 2

THINK ON YOUR FEET

One day, I walked into the showroom of a dealership, ready to pitch my training product. The owner greeted me with a look of frustration. As I offered my hand to introduce myself, he barked for me to follow him to his office. Once inside, he walked across the room to his desk, pulled the top drawer completely out, and dumped hundreds of business cards onto his desk. He then spoke very loudly stating, if I could sell a car to each one of you sons of bitches trying to sell me something, I would make a fortune.

Completely stunned by his dramatic display, I had to remind myself to stay in the moment. This wasn't an objection I was used encountering.

Think Joni. Think **fast.**

I stuck out my arm and, in one dramatic movement, brushed the cards off the desk until each of them landed chaotically in a pile on the floor. I placed my very own business card on top of the now decluttered desk. With confidence, I looked at him square in the face and said if you want the job done right, you've finally met the person that can help you. For as proud as I felt for what I did, his face did not look encouraging.

"Leave immediately," he demanded.

Despite his rejection, when I was standing on the showroom floor moments later, I still had that sense of pride. Well, that took guts, I thought.

Chapter 3 | Suburban Madison

Overall, my young life was filled with certainty and support. Most of what I can remember back then ranges from the orange sherbet push pops we would grab from the corner drug store to laying out in the back yard under our beautiful apple tree with my sisters. I was a carefree little girl with blond, curly hair, completely unaware of all the change that the early '60s brought to the world, and I was happy with that.

At the age of 5, our family moved into the suburbs of Madison, to a town called Westport. It was a newly built home with a large back yard and space for me and my sisters to run. This was a time in my life that felt simple and trusting. A time when television programs ended by midnight, cell phones were non-existent, and instead of using a computer as a vessel for adventure, it was our imagination that propelled us.

In the warmer months, my sisters and I would take to the woods to build forts, or we would venture on a short trip to our cabin at Fish Lake. Our cabin was on the side of the lake where there were hardly any neighbors and no trailers. Mornings at the lake were peaceful, as the owner would set his sheep free and their wake-up calls were one of BAAAHs in unison. The days at the lake were filled with games of hide-and-seek & kick-the-can. On occasion, I remember playing some fun tricks on the younger kids. One time, a couple friends and I thought it would be hilarious to light a firecracker and push it through a crack in the outhouse... while it was being occupied. As the firecracker let out a vicious stream of *cracks* and *pops*, the occupant ran frantically from the outhouse, screaming in shock. Our laughter was short lived when we realized that we were busted. Although, looking back, it was a pretty risky prank, it was hilarious to us.

On the more populated side of the lake were many large trailers, a small game room and bar. It was in the game room that I learned how to play pinball - and that tilting a pinball machine was not smart for a small girl to do. We knew a group of close family-friends that had a trailer on this side of the lake and spent many evenings there-gathered around a warm bonfire, singing songs. One of our favorite songs to sing together was, "Chapel of Love". That song, along with "Jeremiah Was a Bull Frog", still ring clearly in my head. The kids would yell out the words to each song while the parents would enjoy coolers full of beer.

As wonderful as these evenings were, they always came with a precarious ending as my father would drive the boat through the dark, lake air to get us back to our cabin. He liked to stand up while he steered the boat, buzzed from our campfire gathering. Looking at pictures from those days, I always thought he looked a lot like Napoleon leading his army across the waters to battle. I often think back on how lucky we were nothing happened during our boat rides home. Yes, we had life jackets, but that chance of something tragic occurring was certainly possible. The '60s were a time of innocence for our family, and life at the lake was easier.

Back at home, my father loved to BBQ. He would customarily determine how long it was until dinner would be ready based upon how many beers he wanted to drink.

"When are we having dinner?" One of us would ask.

"Two more beers," he would reply.

I remember, one evening as a strong storm blew in, the clouds in the sky became quite dark and ominous. My father looked up at the sky and stated, "that's blacker than Toby's ass". I responded, who's Toby. Awe, that innocence factor again.

-

For children, snow is just as magical as sun. In the Midwestern winters, we flew down hills on toboggans with only lit torches to guide us. Between the layers of socks and scarves, and the rush of racing back up the steep incline, we were able to stay warm despite the frigid wind. These were special evenings. The kind of moments that seemed never ending. Rosy cheeked adults and kids laughing, sledding, giving us a reason to love winter. We were all kids who knew how life was patterned. We would build things with our hands and imaginations, and wait a year to see our favorite movie, The Wizard of Oz. This way of life was embraced and accepted because we didn't know any different. This was a time when experiencing joyous moments meant waiting or working hard. There is no denying that the delay in gratification made the end-result taste even sweeter.

My love for spending time outdoors was magnified when my father taught me to ride a bike. His technique was risky, but efficient. He simply ran beside me and pushed me down a hill. I got the hang of it quickly- I had no choice at the speed I was going. While frightening at first, I found it liberating. Knowing how to ride a bike meant I now had my own means of transportation. Those first solo trips were thrilling. I finally had a way to buy my favorite "Big Mouth" gum (I believe they called it "Big Mouth" because of the size, and I had a very large mouth to accommodate it).

In hindsight, my affinity for outdoor activities was hilarious considering the fact that I lacked basic coordination and possessed sub-par athletic skills. I was the type of baseball player that, when called up to bat, the entire outfield took 5 giant steps closer to the infield. My teammates would indiscreetly gather their gloves, so they could be ready to take the field once I struck out. None of this was too encouraging.

I would certainly describe myself as a tomboy back in those days. You see, girls just were not the common thread for sports and athletics- not like today. And, while some of my sisters enjoyed spending their time on indoor activities- building the skillset of a '60s housewife, I consistently had the urge to be moving, scraping my knees and getting into trouble. Luckily, my middle sister, Jackie, shared this similar interest.

It was at this care-free time in my life that I earned several accurate nicknames including; Potato, Pumpkin, Donut and Sunshine. These nicknames perfectly highlighted my love for food and fun. Perhaps that is part of the reason for the title of this book! I have always looked at life as a gift. I believe it is this mindset that has helped make me successful and, at times, fearless.

–

Our lives in Westport made us students of St. Mary's of the Lake Catholic School. Unlike my first day of kindergarten, my first couple of years in grade school went smoothly. The nuns were called mothers, and they were structured and kind. We could feel that they genuinely wanted us to succeed.

The primary priest was Monsignor Auchter. After my first solo singing performance at church, he dubbed me with a new nickname, "The Belter". I loved to sing. As a 6-year-old girl, I would stand in front of our congregation at Sunday mass and sing, acapella (without music). Our priest would put a big smile on his face, walk down to where I stood singing and move me back from the microphone, bringing chuckles to the congregation. I felt right at home at the center of attention.

One day in school, we were all brought to the cafeteria for an eye exam. As I stood in line and looked at the chart, I was surprised to realize that I couldn't read anything! Panicking, I turned to my best friend, Terri, who was standing beside me, and begged for her to lend me her glasses. As the line progressed, I memorized the first few rows. Just as I approached the front of the line, they moved me to a new position. I could not believe it. I stared at the chart which was a fuzzy blur of letters.

Walking home that day from school, I was so nervous to tell my parents the result of the exam. My father was angry. He took a strong hold of my arm and guided me into the kitchen. He instructed me to read the words that were displayed on our refrigerator door. I couldn't.

The next day, we went to pick up glasses. The walls were lined with pairs of glasses, and my eyes were immediately drawn to a pair of pink glasses with rhinestones. I'm sure you could imagine my excitement when I ended up with a pair of plain black ones. Once I put the glasses on, though, it didn't matter what they looked like. I was completely overwhelmed at the colors and scenery I had been missing. In my young mind, I thought my dad was upset because I failed my vision test, but I think the unexpected expense is what took him most by surprise.

Stories from the Road: Number 3

YUGO FIND ME MORE SALES

I had a client in a small town in Tennessee who was a Yugo dealer. To give you an idea of the quality of this vehicle, it ranks on TIME Magazine's list of 50 worst cars of all time. TIME and author Dan Neil, a Pulitzer Prize-winning automotive critic, describe this vehicle as "having the distinct feeling of something assembled at gunpoint." Regardless, the dealer and I came up with a great campaign idea to sell 72 Yugos in 72 hours. I got to work training sales people and hiring appointment setters to drive as much traffic to the dealership as possible.

The day finally came and customers started to arrive.

The dealership, placed in the valley between two large hills, was swarming with people anxious to test drive. The Yugo was notably bad at accelerating due to its low power. As test drives turned out of the dealership parking lot and began climbing the hills to either side, we noticed the vehicles began to struggle- Some were even rolling completely backwards. Many people came back from their test drives – understandably, with a change of heart – and informed us that they were no longer interested in buying a Yugo. Some customers were more polite than others when announcing their displeasure with the car. Many keys were hurled, many unkind words were spoken. And yet, by some miracle, at the end of the day we sold 77 units!

A couple of short weeks later that number dwindled to a whopping 50 following multiple returns, but hey, we gave it a strong effort!

Chapter 4 | Above the Tavern

In our early days, as a family, we would occasionally stay at my father's childhood home above the tavern. My grandparents typically limited our sleepovers to one child at a time, as that was all they could handle. I found these visits to be stressful. Their home felt eerie, especially knowing I wasn't surrounded by my usual gaggle of siblings. A visit to my grandparents' house did have its perks, though. We were given ten cents toward any item in their convenience store. My oldest sister used her money towards butter- random, I know- she didn't believe in the use of margarine in the way my mother did. My other middle sister was the saver. She built up a small bank of dimes with each visit. I, on the other hand, used every penny of my stipend towards candy. My youngest sister simply flashed her smile and got whatever items she desired. Recounting this story today, I believe one can tell a lot about a child's future by the way they spend their allowance.

When it was my night to stay over, I would lie in bed, under the open window, with a belly full of candy and listen to the cars drive by. As the push and pull of the wind made the curtain dance, I would think about how lonely my father must have been growing up there. It was a strange to feel alone while hearing the constant buzz of patrons below, laughing as they filled themselves with drink and food.

-

On Christmas Eve, when the whole family gathered above the tavern, we would be taking our baths, and hear a loud, "HO! HO! HO!" Reindeer bells jingled, and my sisters and I would scatter quickly to try and get our pajamas on in time to see Santa. We never made it out in time to see who had put the presents around the tree, but I always had a sneaking suspicion it was my grandfather because he had the most Christmas spirit. Whoever played Santa always made sure there presents under the tree for each of us.

My grandfather, Bill, was a kind person. He always smelled of whisky and had an easy demeanor around my sisters and me. During the days I spent above the tavern, he and I would go out to the garden and dig up potatoes and other vegetables. He shared stories from his childhood, which was a sharp contrast to my grandmother, Catherine, who shared very little with us. I supposed hearing stories from his life made us feel closer to him. Once I became an adult, I would learn that he had lived as a functioning alcoholic. With that new found knowledge, I now could see why my grandmother was a more closed or disappointed person.

I was young when my grandfather passed away. He was 64. His funeral was the place where I saw my father cry for the first time. It's hard to forget the first time we see loved ones cry, but it was especially impactful for me. My father, being as stern as he was, had never shown this type of vulnerability. Seeing him let his guard down made me realize that there was a loving man under his cold exterior. In a strange way, the image of my father crying allowed me to feel more comfortable opening up to him. From that moment on, no matter how tough he would get as a parent, I knew that my father was a loving person.

Naturally with my grandfather's passing, my grandmother had also been greatly affected. As the years went by, she grew to be a gentler person. She sold their business and decided to move into her own home. No doubt this was a tough step for her, but, for once in her life, she didn't have to work so physically hard. It's funny- in a sad way- that people often hold back from living their lives to the fullest until something, or someone, is taken from them.

-

During this time, on my mother's side, things were not entirely blissful, either. My grandmother Rose died of breast cancer shortly before I was born. She was taken quickly by the awful disease and left two very young children, along with a broken man. Her death was so devastating to my grandfather, Ambrose, that he quickly married what appeared to be the first woman he met. Unfortunately, he met her in a bar, where the lighting must've been very poor and -I can only assume- he was heavily intoxicated.

My description may seem harsh, but Dorothy was a cruel and destructive person. She was the polar opposite of my grandmother. From every conversation I was a part of, it appeared that she made it her mission to hurt people. Both physically and mentally. My mom's siblings, Aunt Kathe and Uncle Scott, were scarred beyond repair because of the time they spent with Dorothy. Unsure of what true love was, both Kathe and Scott would spend their entire lives searching aimlessly for something that would fill the hole Dorothy left in them.

As I grew older, I could not help but look closely at my grandfather and recognize how much he had let his children down. It was so sad. He could not prioritize his own kids, so when my grandmother passed away, it wasn't one life that was lost, but four.

Stories from the Road: Number 4

PAID TO DRINK

I traveled to a new account in Portsmouth, New Hampshire when I was 27 years old. It was at this store that I made a lifelong friend, Tanya. Tanya was also 27 and was the sales manager for the store. The purpose of my visit was to train the sales team and ensure the training was turned into action.

Dick was the owner of the dealership and one of the most eccentric people I had ever met. He fought in the Vietnam War, and I had to surmise that some of his personality traits were a direct result of that experience.

At the time, my daily fee at was $1500, and despite this fact, it was not uncommon for Dick to interrupt a training session and tell me to grab my coat. You see, he loved to sit in a dark bar and regale about stories from the past. I would sip slowly on a cold beer while he wasted no time downing his cocktails. It was the first time I had ever been paid $1500 per day to drink with someone. I was always known to be a good listener, but this was taking it to a new level!

I felt lucky to be in his good graces because he was known for having a quick temper. One day, he was arguing with a customer on the lot, in clear sight of everybody in the dealership. The customer kept repeating the words, "Cheaper! Cheaper!"

Dick took the customers head and slammed it onto the hood of the car. "Now it's cheaper!"

I had to put together an apology script for when Dick lost his temper around a customer. Between our "therapy" sessions at the bar and the apology calls to customers, I would say that $1500 per day was money well spent.

Chapter 5 | Our First Major Move

When I was nine, my father received a promotion that landed us in Jefferson City, Missouri. Though I was sad to leave my friends, and had no idea where Missouri fell on a map, I remember feeling the move provided me with a sense of an adventure.

Our new home was at the base of a tall hill, which meant new adventures for bike riding. The backyards on our block all adjoined, and my dad quickly found new friends to join in his favorite game of horse shoes. On special Sunday evenings, we would enjoy cooking "tube steaks" (my Dad's term for hot dogs) over the fire in our downstairs fireplace; and we added a new family member, our dog, Dutch, who had short legs, but out-ran even the biggest of dogs when chased.

At the time, I was just old enough to begin my career in babysitting and I started on a mission to save money for important items such as a fringe suede vest, a new bathing suit, and a pair of 'clackers'. For all the young folks out there that derive all their entertainment from electronic devices, clackers were glass balls connected on a string and would "clack" when they hit each other- an unsafe concept, to say the least.

My entrepreneurial interests also afforded me the funds to purchase a bright pink baby doll style bathing suit from Montgomery Ward. Montgomery Ward was a popular department store, similar to what Macy's is today. I was *so* proud that I managed to save enough to afford that bathing suit. I waited anxiously all year for when the public pool would finally open. When it finally did, there I was; wearing my brand-new pink suit, ready to show the world who was in charge. I jumped into the water and splashed around, my new neighborhood friends, Julie and Karen, by my side. As I came to the surface of the water, they both pointed out a trail of pink behind me. I quickly kicked my way to the edge and jumped out of the pool to assess the damage.

Where my suit used to be a bright, lively pink, it was now nearly completely white. I rushed over to my Mom, flustered at the events that had just unfolded.

"Look!" I urged with tears in my eyes. I worked hard to earn this swimsuit, and I wanted her to share in my frustration. *Certainly*, I thought, *we should return it.*

But she didn't seem concerned. At a time when my young, broken heart could have used a little empathy, my mom peered up at me from her pool chair and said, "It looks fine in white."

Luckily for me, she couldn't hear my response as I carefully muttered my disappointment under my breath.

While my investments in material goods seemed to consistently fall through, I had my matchbook collection hobby to fall back on. It was a time where smoking was still acceptable, and I enjoyed grabbing matchbooks from local businesses that all strived to show their own personal brand. I kept my eye out for new matchbooks everywhere we went. One day, I showed my Mom and Dad a unique matchbook that I had found along the road. It turned out this matchbook I was so proud of was a package of condoms. Their laughing still echoes in my head. I didn't know what was so funny about my new discovery.

The new school my sisters and I attended was a Catholic school, much like in Westport. This school was led by "the Sisters of Mercy", a name which I found ironic considering they didn't take any mercy on me. On my first day of school, the sister that led my class asked me to stand and introduced me to the class as JOHNNY.

As all kids with unusual spellings know, mispronunciation is a standard part of life, so I politely corrected her, "My name is pronounced Joannie."

"Well, it's spelled like Johnny, so that is what we are going to call you", she replied.

The class laughed and, it was at that moment, that I decided I hated her.

Our school uniforms were forest green. My mom found a sweater on sale that was very obviously *NOT* forest green. It was more of a pea green- that green, yellow, brown combination that reminds you of bad cafeteria food. I was *already* a young girl being called by a boy's name. I had no interest in standing out any more than I already did. I voiced my concern about the sweater being the wrong color, but my mom quickly dismissed me. "It's close enough." She said.

Here comes Johnny with her pea green sweater.

In 5th grade, I entered the school's talent show to sing, "Cecelia" by Simon and Garfunkel. I imagine most children don't understand the meanings behind many of their favorite lyrics- I was certainly one of them. This song talks about "making love". I did my first stint in Catholic school detention shortly after the performance.

Due to my outspoken and fearless nature (at least, that's how I'd like to think of it), I landed myself in trouble more than once at this point in my life. One day, in class, I felt the nun was treating one of my classmates unfairly. I spoke up. The nun directed me to the front of the class where she proceeded to slap my cheek. "Turn the other cheek, as it states in the bible," she urged.

"No way," I replied.

A short time later I was sitting in detention, yet again.

Our school was led by Monsignor Pelker. He was such an ego-maniac that whenever he entered the room, we had to stop what we were doing, stand and immediately break into song- singing a song he had written about himself.

No matter how bizarre or absurd the school seemed to us, our mother never believed our experiences at the Sisters of Mercy Catholic School. Usually, after airing our grievances, she would snap back at us with, "What did you do wrong to deserve this?" My mother was old school and, to this day, continues to be blinded by the Irish brogue.

Whatever her reasons, my mother's lack of support has stayed with me my entire life. It was a bitter pill that I had refused to swallow for quite some time, but I learned that, though my mother was a part of our family, my sisters and I were really on our own.

Apart from the dread that came from school, our family's experience in the state of Missouri was actually enjoyable. My parents made new lifelong friendships and, as a family, we often explored the Ozarks and beautiful rivers. During warm summer days, my dad and mom would drop us off at the same river bank and give us all a flimsy, rubber inner tube. My sisters and I, ranging from 4 to 14 floated for several miles, without any adult supervision, to meet our parents at a sandbar. Thankfully, none of us drowned!

It has become a classic trope in parenting that, for you to let your kids grow up, you need allow them to fail. Some parents start teaching this lesson by taking the bumpers off in a game of bowling or taking the training wheels off a child's bike. My parents preferred to throw us right in the deep end. For example, when my father taught us how to ride a bike, he would take a running head start and shove us forward. "You fall, you get back up."

Perhaps his approach taught me resiliency.

On sunny days, my older sisters and I laid out on foil mats and lathered up with our concoction of baby oil and iodine. I wasn't quite sure why this was important, however I wanted to fit in and be part of their world. It was while we laid out together, that I could be privy to their conversations. A lot of discussion surrounded boys they liked. The topics really didn't matter, though. What was important to me was simply being included. I was still young, but I learned from my sisters that being tan was cool, so tan I would be.

Our couple years in Jefferson City forced us all out of our comfort zones. It was all about meeting new people and finding a way to fit in. Our parents hosted frequent parties and BBQs, so their friends' children quickly became our friends, too. My middle sister Jackie and I took piano lessons, from a teacher named Mrs. Ziffle. Obviously, from assumptions with that name, we were not taught fun current music, but rather Mozart and other greats. I also found a passion for playing the drums. My parents ignored my plea for a drum set one Christmas, and instead brought a drum pad. It seems, in order to excel at an instrument, it takes time and practice. None of which I had or applied. When the time came to show my drum skills at our Spring Music Recital, I stood up on stage, completely clueless on how to read the sheet music, and proceeded to drum away. Although many of the audience and band members were confused, I thought it sounded great.

Shockingly, I wasn't asked back to join the next recital...

But to hell with of the outcome of my drumming career, I thought. As far as I was concerned, I had accomplished our family mission of trying new things in Jefferson City. I learned that I am extremely comfortable being uncomfortable, and this is a trait that would carry far in life.

Stories from the Road: Number 5

FLEXIBILITY IS KEY

One account I had was in a small-town in Louisiana. Upon arrival, I got to my room and started to unpack. Much to my dismay, I realized I had packed two completely different shoes- one cream, one black.

The small town did not have any open stores where I could buy a new, matching pair of shoes, so, the next morning, I went to my client's dealership with mismatched shoes and didn't say a word.

I carefully observed people's reactions, laughing at their subtle attempts not to stare too long. Finally, one person finally felt secure enough to ask me about my peculiar fashion choice.

"It's all the rage in Chicago," I said confidently.

I wonder if I started any trends in that town after my visit.

Chapter 6 | Home Sweet Omaha

In the late spring of 1971, my father received another promotion- this time to Omaha, Nebraska. His position with the Tobacco company was thriving, and he was promoted to District Manager. This was a difficult transition for my oldest sister, who was just finding her footing in high school, but I was thrilled to leave "Johnny" and the tough Irish nuns behind.

The rigid structure of our home life continued in Omaha. My father arrived home from work and spent an hour sipping cocktails and talking with my mother. We were not allowed to interrupt them during this time- it was forbidden. My dad desperately needed this one on one time with my mom.

At precisely 5:30 PM each evening, we would sit down for dinner. At this age, my sisters and I knew what behaviors were acceptable at the dinner table, but my oldest sister had this ridiculous habit of sitting on her feet; A habit my father was determined to break. Through ridicule and mean comments, my father slowly broke my sister down. Being the breadwinner, my dad was able to get away with a lot. My mother would look down at her plate and move her food around with her fork, my other sisters followed her lead, but I was the child with a voice that was not afraid to use it. "Why don't you pick on someone your own age", I said. And before I could finish my sentence, I was whisked out of my chair and thrown against the refrigerator. My father despised being challenged, yet I always saw something in his eyes that told me he was proud of my tenacity.

-

I continued my middle school education in the Catholic school system. The nuns were much more kind than what I had known in Missouri, and one of our priests was extremely handsome. When confession day rolled around, I confessed that I had crush on him. Three Hail Marys later, I was forgiven for my crush.

In 1972, I was entering the 8thgrade, and a new busing trial occurred, which mandated busing for certain students. I lived in a bubble for my entire life, and this busing trial was the first time I sat alongside an African American.

In the evenings, I would often play basketball with my next-door neighbor. He was Jewish. I remember telling him how sorry I was that he would not go to heaven. I realize now how naïve and sheltered I was for all those years. I was exposed to more diversity my first year in Omaha, than any other time in my life.

Outside of the classroom, I decided to quench my thirst for attention by trying out for cheerleading. I was no gymnast, but I was loud and I could get a crowd involved. So, I made the team!

At the same time, I continued expanding my resume by doing labor jobs in our neighborhood. My middle sister and I mowed lawns and shoveled snow. The only catch was that we had to sell our services before our mother got involved, otherwise she would sell our services in exchange for cookies.

I graduated 8th grade feeling excitement for the next chapter in my life. That day, on the risers of our graduation stage, I sang my final song as a middle schooler. Under my wire-rimmed glasses was a bright eyes girl, and under my straight brown hair (yes, my blonde curls disappeared), was a head full of dreams.

I was enrolled in a public school for 9th grade. Nothing can prepare a young, sheltered girl for the shock that comes along with transitioning from a Catholic school environment to that of a public school. A girl in my class was pregnant, there was a classmate with a full beard, and my fellow cheerleaders told me that if I wanted to get a boyfriend, I had to have sex. I was mortified. I had never even kissed a boy yet. Besides, the nuns told us that our bodies were a temple. I knew I could not talk with my mom about this, so I felt lonely and scared. I can tell you that I did get a boyfriend, with zero sex. I think he was as frightened by growing up, as I was.

Cheerleading continued to be my "sport" in high school. After 9th grade, I was registered at a local high school. The cheer squad cheered at nearly every game, which definitely helped with my limited wardrobe because I got to wear my uniform to school every day.

At the beginning of high school, I decided that when it came to my year book, I wanted to have the largest list of committees and groups under my name: Future Homemakers of America, Choir, Swing Choir, Drama, Newspaper, Track, Golf; You name it, I did it.

Both my sister and I tried out for the same role in Drama Club's Jesus Christ Superstar. I sang my audition song acapella and *nailed* it. In fact, I was *so* good that, when the song finished, my sister ran out crying. The director came up to me and privately asked to me consider letting my sister have the role. You see, she was a senior, and I was a sophomore. Giving up this part was easy.

I love my sister, and her happiness meant so much more than being in the role. The following year, I secured the main role in the play Medea. (who in the world would pick a Greek tragedy for a high school play?) On opening night, my parents were sitting center front row. As I recited my lines, I could not help but smile as I caught a glimpse of my father, sound asleep.

No matter how preoccupied I was with my extracurriculars, my father was very clear that I needed to keep my grades up. Out of pure fear of reprimand, I excelled in all classes and was in the National Honors Society throughout my high school years. I remember meeting with my guidance counsellor and asking her, "What would be the best steps for taking over the world?"

My father felt that the best move for all of us was to just get a "basic job"- 9-5, Monday thru Friday. I think he loved the idea of us being a grocery store checkout person or a secretary. *Yikes*, that did not exactly align with my goal to take over the world.

My sophomore year of high school, my older sister, then 19, became engaged to be married. Let's face it, after approximately three weeks of dating anyone, you could put money on the fact that my mother would be laying out the "good china" and planning our weddings. Because of their successful, whirlwind romance, our parents not only wanted, but expected, the same for all of us. It is a rarity that anyone who only knew someone for six weeks, could end up in a stable and loving relationship for life. It's just not the norm. This mentality typically pushed my sisters and I into less than suitable relationships. We were simply trying to please our parents.

Feeling the pressure, I began dating a boy from my high school. He was a junior, kind and mellow. He was the youngest in his family with much older siblings and did not share in any of the relationship pressures my parents put on us. We dated for a couple of years and, while my girlfriends were receiving jewelry for presents, I received a pet bird. I had no idea what to do with a pet bird, so I tried my best to, at least, feed him and keep him alive. One day, while my younger sister was at home, she set the bird cage down onto a chair and forgot about him. Later that day I came home to find a pile of feathers and our dog, Rags, nearby with a big smile on her face.

I couldn't blame our dog, but I had to come up with a quick solution. After a trip to a nearby pet store, I purchased a replacement bird. Though not the same bright yellow, I thought it was close enough. It brought a smile to my face whenever my boyfriend would remark how the bird's feathers were slightly changing colors. Go figure.

During our time in Omaha, my parents purchased a tiny cottage and boat on a lake approximately 40 miles away. It was there that I learned to love water skiing. My father would take me out solo, and as I sped across the water, I found it a most appropriate time to start singing songs at the top of my lungs. This was a very narrow lake, and didn't realize that my vocals were entertaining (or disturbing) the host of other cabin owners. Our evenings were spent sitting around a campfire and, to this day, I can still hear the crackling of the logs and the smell of the fire. Our small cabin at the lake offered our family a wonderful bit of refuge. But, as teenage years must possess some elements of screw ups, I had a great one while at this very lake.

My mother had planned a cook out with several co-workers for a beautiful summer day. My girlfriend and I were instructed to stay at the entrance and let people in as they arrived at the gate. It was a scorching-hot summer day in Nebraska, and so the thought of a cold beer seemed far too tempting. The local grocer, who was an old man that could not care less about how old we were, was the ideal location to make our purchase. We figured that he probably started drinking beer himself around the age of 10.

That hot day passed by, and as the last guests arrived, we finally got back into our vehicle to head to the cabin, desperately needing to use the bathroom. In my buzzed state of mind, I made the rather stupid decision to drive the car slowly, right up the small, sandy beach and into the lake. As we opened the car doors, the water rushed in. Our laughter was uncontrollable.

As fate would have it, being cute girls, some of the nearby boys came swiftly to our rescue. In no time at all, the car was back out of the lake, and there was no true damage done. That next morning, I realized how damn lucky I was that my father never found out about that crazy decision.

-

In 1975 was hit by a devastating tornado Omaha. On that dreadful evening, guess which lucky girl was chosen to drive her cheerleading squad to the shop and grab their new uniforms? This location was over 45 minutes from my home, so once the sirens started blaring and the sky became pitch black, I knew we could be in real danger. Beginning to panic, I can remember thinking that our best move would be drive as fast as possible without ever looking back. But as time progressed and we passed several cars stuck in the ditches, we began to hear the eerie sound of the wind become increasingly audible. I have no idea how, but we made it to my house that afternoon. The trip had been so overwhelming that I might as well have blacked out. As we ran to the basement, I made sure to grab peanut butter, bread and a radio. We huddled together and listened to the loud, strange sounds of the wind and rain that seemed to last forever. Once everything seemed to subside, we walked outside to see a frightening path of debris. Our home was not severely harmed, but the houses across the street were devastated. The tornado spared us and devoured those nearby. We all helped to assist everyone less fortunate than us, however, it would take years for the community to not only rebuild, but to forget.

My high school years offered quite a change from the days of Catholic school. There were no less than 25% African American students enrolled in our school. With the diverse student body, the school had two styles of bands: Traditional and Harambee. Quite frankly, I would much rather have been able to march to the fun beat of Harambee, rather than the slow sounds of the band, "Chicago". But there was a silent division here. Nothing anyone discussed. Conversations were always one of unity yet race clearly built an invisible wall. I remember one year, as prom was approaching, the quarterback from our football team, who was black, asked me to the dance. When my parents heard of this invitation, they quickly told me not to accept it. Because of their response, I realized that, while they promoted equality through their words, their true emotions told a different story.

High school was flying by. With all the commitments and increasing social activities, I could not believe how quickly senior year was approaching.

I was fired from my first part time job at a small local restaurant for giving away a free hamburger. It took me by surprise because everyone gave away free food to friends, but the manager, who was a vile, flirtatious man, knew that I could not tolerate him. I believe that is why he let me go. *Good riddance*, I thought. This experience started another pathway towards my career view point: Never, ever tolerate that what is intolerable.

As I started to look at another avenue for income, a friend of mine told me about the seasonal work of corn-shucking. From verbal description, the hourly rate seemed good for what seemed to be a simple job. *Wow*, was I wrong. The job was very physically demanding. The summers in Nebraska are notably hot, and walking through corn fields in the Nebraska summer heat was stifling. Beyond the smothering heat, the stalks were very sharp. It was necessary, in this line of work, to dress in long sleeves to protect your skin, a uniform which made the humidity even more unbearable.

One day, the farmer must have forgotten we were in the fields and turned on the irrigation system. As the fields started to flood, you could hear the screams of the other migrant workers running and yelling in Spanish. Today that scene still makes me chuckle. I ran, along with my team workers, and enjoyed the feel of cool water on my sunburnt skin.

For extra income, I offered to clean the buses we rode in to and from the fields for an extra $5.00. Yes, I had work ethic even back then.

The corn shucking job was summers only, so I searched for additional revenue. My sister, Jackie, was working at a dime store in a nearby mall. She was a cashier, and I was hired initially to work in the candy department. One day, I noticed the popcorn machine needed cleaning. I took it upon myself to take on this task. Using ammonia, I had it sparkling. I'm sure you can only imagine the smell of popcorn and ammonia filling the store. Regardless of my good intentions, the machine was ruined, and I was demoted to stocking. This was a long part time job, and I would fill with envy when I would take a break and walk by my sister, who was always smiling at her cashier stand, the dream role for anybody working at the dime store.

When it came time to decide on a college, I knew I wanted to leave Omaha. I was ready to blaze my own trail in the world and knew a change in location was key.

My grades and involvement in so many activities made my application attractive to many universities. So, I applied and was accepted to the University of Wisconsin-Madison.

As I sat on graduation day, listening to over 650 names of fellow students, I realized how few people I had gotten to know in those past three years.

My parents took my sisters and I out for a celebratory dinner- a rare occurrence in our family- and gifted me a new suitcase. I saw this as their subtle message to say, *Go.*

The next day I packed up my belongings, and my pet bird, and left Omaha behind me, ready to start the next chapter in my life.

Stories from the Road: Number 6

OH, CANADA

By the time I had several years of consulting experience, I took my talents international and was booked to go to Canada. The line for customs slowly progressed forward, and, when it was my turn, I made my way to the next available agent.

When asked if my visit was for pleasure or business, I proudly responded, "Business."

They then asked for the proper documentation or visa to enter and conduct this work. I had none. I was whisked into a private room where I sat for hours until I was finally allowed access into the country.

After experiencing this hassle, I chose to avoid Canada visits for years. In fact, it was nearly 20 years later that I accepted an invitation to speak in Winnipeg. The client assured me that all I needed to do was advise customs that I was visiting a friend. "It's super easy," he said.

As I approached customs, I strategically selected the person I thought would be easiest to convince. In my baseball hat and jeans, I walked up to the counter.

"What is your purpose for visiting?" the agent asked.

"To visit a friend." I stated, confidently.

"What friend?" she asked.

I paused, which, by the way, is the telltale sign of lying. I slowly responded with a first name.

"Where does he live?" she asked.

So. Many. Questions! By now, I was stuck. I was whisked, once again, back into the private room for further questioning, with not so much as a window to stare out. They demanded my laptop and passwords. The questioning became serious, and I kept thinking, I was just there to help a client handle their phone calls effectively!

When they asked me if I had ever killed anyone, I knew my lie had gone on way too long. I finally broke down and admitted I was there for work.

My admission didn't go over well. The customs agent took my passport and required I stay at the airport until the next flight back to Chicago.

The next morning, as the United Airline customers stood up waiting to board the flight, I was escorted by two Canadian Mounties to the gate. Whispers and looks ran rampant. I had to laugh to myself. I thought Canadians were nice.

Chapter 7 | College Girl

As I started my new life in Madison, I felt like Mary Tyler Moore in *That Girl.* The only problem was I didn't have a job. I did, however, have a couple good friends, and the first couple weeks being on my own was exhilarating. But then, it was time to get serious. My parents did not provide me with any financial assistance, so I was completely on my own.

I read that the local newspaper employees were on strike, and as a direct result of this, they were hiring. I crossed that picket line in my orange VW Bug as the picketers threw rocks at me. Quite frankly, I really didn't care that I was being a "scab". I had bills to pay; and tuition; and living expenses. Bottom line is, I needed the work.

That afternoon, I was hired for classified advertising and, as an extra bonus, I took death notices on weekends and holidays. Undoubtedly, writing death notices put a damper on what should have been fun Saturdays spent at college football games. One thing I learned is that people are very picky when it comes to proper spelling of names in those darn notices. It was sometimes difficult to keep my composure when I would have a family come in and say things like, "My Aunt passed away *unexpectedly* at the age of 95."

I could not help but think, *Really? Unexpectedly?*

Far too often, I made small errors and found myself in the manager's office on Monday mornings being reprimanded. I imagine it wasn't easy to find someone to take over that weekend and holiday work, so therefore I remained. In fact, I worked at the newspaper throughout my entire time in school.

At one point, I even took on another job at a local family restaurant. I was never one with great waitressing skills, so I worked in the bar. I will never forget one evening when an elderly gentleman offered me $20 just to dance one song with him. As I took that $20, I realized I was perhaps at one of my lowest financial points. Let's face it. Rent, Tuition, Life, Car Parking, Insurance- all of it was expensive. It was at this point in my life when I swore that if I ever became a parent, I would never put my kids through this. I would make sure they had a FUN college experience- the way it always looked in the movies.

My sophomore year of college, my father decided to retire back to Madison. The tobacco companies were coming under siege with warnings and tobacco-related health issues. I believe it was the feeling of being forced to hire with equality that really pushed my dad into early retirement. In any event, it was good to have the family back and close by.

Unfortunately, news of them coming back to Madison came at a bittersweet time, as a dear friend of mine from Omaha, Cheryl, passed away. We had met in 7th grade and been friends from that point on. Poor Cheryl was diagnosed with Hodgkin's disease in 8th grade. She had been fighting cancer for years, so her death was not one of shock, but still of great sadness. I told my parents that I was going to drive back to Omaha for the funeral. I never understood why, but my father forbade me to go. So, with that in mind, I went.

My trusty VW took me the 400 miles to Omaha. It was so surreal to look at a 19-year-old friend in a casket. Nothing really prepares you for that. I cried and shared an evening with my friends; Reminiscing on what is good in life.

The next day, I woke up super early to start my journey back to Madison. It was still dark- and very cold outside- as I hit the highway. I remember thinking how peaceful the world was. Just outside of town as I neared Council Bluffs, my check engine light came on. At the time, the VW Bug had an air-cooled engine and you absolutely had to keep adequate oil in it. I had always been very diligent about this, however when the light came on, I realized the last gas station must not have checked the levels. With all this racing through my mind, my car came to a jolting stop. In a fit of punches, I hit my steering wheel hard enough to hear the ferocious "BEEP" of my car horn. Thanks to my talent for being uncoordinated at moments, one of my flailing fists knocked right into my glasses. *CRACK!* I climbed out of my car to assess the damage under the hood, I bent down to release the latch and heard a *RIP* from my skirt. This day could not get any worse.

With no real options, I hitched a ride to the closest truck stop and called my parents. Just sitting in the stranger's car, I could not help but feel frightened and disappointed at the world that day. I lost a dear friend *AND* I was stranded.

As I explained the series of unfortunate events to my father, he responded in a way that I would never forget, "You made your bed, now lie in it." The dial tone came through the other end, and I knew I was in trouble. No phone, no credit card, no cash. I needed to find a solution.

Turns out you can't do much without money, so I sure hoped my years of church going and confessions would protect me through the next 8 hours of hitchhiking back to Madison. The hours I spent in strangers' cars that day gave me a lot of time to reflect. I consider myself lucky that I met a good couple to take me on the journey. As I watched the highway miles fly by, I could not help but think I would never choose to put somebody I love in the path of danger. How could I ever forgive my parents? Was this act even forgivable to begin with?

I made it home hours later, but I didn't return a phone call to my parents for over a week. I wanted them to worry. I wanted them to think, even for one minute, that they did something wrong. They never said they were sorry or acknowledged that they were wrong. When I did finally return their calls, the conversations were trivial. They would let me know about upcoming family events or ask for information about another family member. Never did either one ever apologize. This bothers me even as I write this many years later.

In his retirement, my father opened a local liquor store in Madison. He offered me a job working several hours a week at a good hourly rate, so I jumped on it. This also became a new outlet for my friends and I to meet people. For example, if someone came over to pick up a keg for a party, we would let them know they only could have it, if we were invited. Also, my friends were known to sit in the back room, enjoying drinks, while I worked at the cash register.

I met a new boyfriend at this store. He came in to pick up his keg and wore a neck bandana with clogs. I found this to be quite cool. Unfortunately, as it came to be, we had absolutely nothing in common, which, in hindsight, is why I was attracted to him in the first place.

As college kids do, I found my fair share of trouble. This was my time to make mistakes and learn from them. My friend and I agreed to volunteer as leaders for my little sister's 8th grade girl scout troupe. Our mandatory training class was held in Chicago, and as exciting as a girl scout training sounded, my uncle's band happened to be playing in the Chicago area that same night; So, we skipped the training and followed the fun. This was probably the first step towards what would inevitably be our impeachment. For several months, we raised money to take the girls to a weekend at a nearby dude ranch. The girls were so excited that day we took off. Perhaps even more excited when my girlfriend and I handed them each a whistle to put around their neck. "If you need us, blow your whistle, we'll be by the pool."

Thank God no one was injured that weekend as those 8th grade girls ran free, while my co-leader and I sat near the pool flirting with the other young ranch workers. Between the dude ranch fiasco and the fact that we were instructing the young women how to apply makeup and what the best songs and dances were, we upset most- if not all- of the troupe parents. They all gathered together to have us removed. Yikes, add impeached girl scout leader to my resume.

Life continued to move and change for myself and family. My oldest sister's marriage began to fall apart. It came to light that, during their engagement, my sister began to see red flags and expressed concerns about getting married to my mother. She shared with me later, that her heart was set on breaking off the engagement, however my mother urged her to go through with the union. After all, the invitations had already been mailed out and this seemed more important than her own daughter's happiness.

During their marriage. my sister and her husband had tried to conceive a child unsuccessfully. As crushing as this was, she found out shortly before her divorce that he had conceived a child with another woman. That betrayal from her first husband truly left her scarred- even today. Their marriage only lasted a few years, and the break up would be the first of many for my sisters and me.

With college and all my jobs keeping me at a pace of 80 hours of work per week, my sister Jackie and I decided to move into an apartment together. She worked at a popular radio station and sang in a local band. Every chance I got, I would be there for her, singing along and dancing with my infamous coordination. I don't think it's a tough picture to paint. Jackie and I are forever bonded in a way that is difficult do describe. We just... are.

As school progressed, my circle of friends at work and school grew. Among them, was a person who shared my unique sense of humor and insight. His name was Scott. We developed a friendship that grew stronger than I ever expected, and naturally, we began dating. It was not necessarily a relationship filled with passion, but it was one built more on comradery.

Scott was a couple years ahead of me in school and had started his initial career in the Milwaukee area. Shortly after graduation, I sought out my first "real job", and landed a gig at the Milwaukee Journal newspaper making $17,500.00 per year. I thought I was rich! I knew I was placed on this earth to make a difference, and my new job was going to help me do just that. Scott and I moved in together, and as he focused on his career, I embraced new opportunities at the newspaper.

As life was comfortably moving in a new direction, I found out I was pregnant. I don't think Scott ever really thought about being a parent, but, for me, there was no doubt I loved the thought. I had no idea what to do or how to do it, but I was excited.

With both Scott and I being raised catholic, marriage was inevitable. I sincerely loved how welcoming his parents were to, not only myself, but our new direction. When I broke the news to my parents, they seemed were happy on the surface. While the timing wasn't ideal to them, I think my mom and dad were excited to welcome a grandchild.

Stories from the Road: Number 7

SUPPORT YOURSELF FINANCIALLY

After a long day of training, I met with my client in his office to review the day's progress. With each hour that had passed, I was proud to provide a step by step list of all the changes I had implemented. A big part of training is to ensure that accountability and clear goals are visible.

When my recap was finished, the owner stated, "I'd like to buy you a steak dinner."

I responded, "Can I get chocolates and nylons, too?" My gosh, was it the 1920's again?

I am more than happy to have a celebratory steak dinner, but I can buy.

It's a statement of pride.

Chapter 8 | You're Going to Be a Mom

I was married in a red dress with polka dots. Nearly every new bride chooses white, but I felt red was more suitable. I was 7 months pregnant, and clueless on parenting. My new husband took a job promotion at his retail company to the Crown Point Indiana area. So, with all the physical changes going on, we added in a new place to live-in as well.

We took Lamaze classes and prepared as best we could for parenting. The day my water broke, we rushed to the Catholic hospital where, to my great dismay, the assigned birthing room nurse was a nun. Yes, in full habit. With every single sharp contraction, I would scream out every four-letter obscenity I could think of. Immediately following that swear word, I would say, "I am so sorry sister".

After 5 hours, I had this beautiful baby completely naturally. As they took me into the delivery room, our doctor was so short, they had to have him stand on a box to reach me. If I wasn't in so much pain, I would have been laughing at the scene.

My first child was a baby boy. Absolutely beautiful. A miracle. For all my life, I thought that I had understood what love was all about. Seeing the way my parents looked at each other, I was convinced that I had seen, and therefore then *known,* what it meant to feel love. It was at that moment, staring into the eyes of my newborn baby boy that I had truly begun to understand what love really means. I knew that I would do anything and everything I could for him.

My next emotions felt like a title wave. How in the world was I equipped to really raise another life? It was so far beyond any financial worries, but rather about being a strong mother for him. During this flurry of anxiety, I received some of the very best advice. My doctor came in and sat beside me. He looked at me and said, "Just love him, the very best you can, one day at a time."

And I can proudly say, I have done just that.

Shortly after the birth of my son, we moved back to Milwaukee where my husband had received another job advancement. We found a large apartment and began to function as a family. My oldest sister was also living in the area and would come by frequently to regale about her new life as a single woman.

I took on a part time job for added income, and still marveled at where my life was at that very moment, compared to where I thought it would be. I began to see very clear differences with regards to how my husband and I viewed the world and the opportunities it offered. For example, if I talked about wanting to go to Hawaii, he'd respond, "We'll never be able to afford that."

While that may seem like a minor difference, to me it was the first major crack in a previously strong foundation.

When our son Ryan was 2 years old, we found out that I was pregnant again. I knew, from the moment I was given this news, that this baby was a little girl. Unlike with my son, I was able to stay with the same physician team and felt much more confident with the entire delivery process. My daughter, Kate, was delivered in only 2 hours. From the first moment she looked into my eyes, to the moments we share today, I can still feel the deep love and bond we share. Its unbendable.

As the days were starting to speed by even more swiftly, I could start to truly sense that my husband was not happy in this world we created. I don't know that fatherhood was his aspiration, rather he just accepted it. Anyone with a strong personality knows how easy it can be to wear down someone with a weaker personality. In many ways, that happened between me and Scott.

Scott's next promotion would take us to a much further location, Syracuse NY. We moved into a townhome and tried to adjust to our new home. One day, I answered the door only to find a sobbing little boy with an angry mother standing there. It appeared that my oldest son, who was a biter, had bitten him for no reason. Not a great way to make friends, but I apologized to the best of my ability and swore he would never do this again. Moving forward, I tried very hard to watch his playing behavior with other kids.

I remember one trip to the Syracuse local grocery store, where I looked up in the produce section and found myself staring right into Richard Gere's face. His family was from this area, and it was not uncommon for him to frequent certain local spots. As I gazed into his penetrating eyes, I could not help but curse my lazy confidence in feeling comfortable to leave home in a sweatshirt and no makeup.

While we lived in Syracuse, my youngest sister became engaged. Her wedding was held approximately 6 months after my daughter, Kate, was born, back in Madison, Wisconsin. Rather than taking on the cost and hassle of multiple flights, Scott and I decided we would drive. The hours of driving meant hours of singing, conversation and gossip. It was clear that Scott was a good friend of mine, but we just lacked the passion of young love.

The wedding was in many ways very happy. My baby sister Jane married a young man she'd met while in high school. They were only 20 years old but professed all the aspects of love. Their wedding was a wonderful evening, and our family felt strongly bonded.

After only 6 months in Syracuse, my husband landed another promotion to Indianapolis, Indiana. The thought of leaving didn't really mean much to any of us. We were both comfortable with change, so we embraced the new opportunity.

As sad as it was to accept, by now my marriage was really one of friendship- not passion. We were a young couple acting as though we were old and in retirement. It was not an acceptable life for myself, but I had a hunch he was comfortable living that way forever. As things became more strained between us, we went to marriage counseling. It was there that I had to share the very difficult reality that I simply wasn't in love with him. My husband's response was one of anger and, quite frankly, I was shocked by this strong emotion. I didn't think he cared that much.

We divorced shortly afterwards, and I had sole custody of my children. Now, the reality of being able to provide for them certainly wasn't going to come from my writing poetry and short stories, so I took a part time job as a waitress at a newly opened Olive Garden. It only took a very short time before I was demoted from a waitress to a bar server. It was at this very establishment that I would meet an interesting group of people who would help start to shape my life in a new direction.

Stories from the Road: Number 8

NEVER CROSS AN 8 MONTH PREGNANT WOMAN

Working in Long Island was tough. The sales team was distinctly more challenging than those from other parts of our country. I was in my third trimester, and my Long Island training workshop was one small part of an east coast tour I committed to with a manufacturer before my son was conceived. Being so far along in my pregnancy, flying was out of the question, so a kind associate was elected as my chauffer. I was 35 years old and had gained 50 pounds during the pregnancy, with feet that had swollen from a size 9 to a 12.

During the course of our travels, I would lay across the back seat of the car. As we'd run through fast food restaurants, I likened myself to some sort of whale, or sea lion that would yelp and have food tossed to them.

At one break during a training session, I overheard several young salespeople from the Long Island area stores complaining about being at the workshop. As the session reconvened, I asked the attendees to raise their hands if they didn't want to be there. Half of the class raised theirs, and I asked them to leave.

"You can't do that" the manufacturer rep said frantically.

Well, I just did. Never cross an 8-month pregnant woman.

Chapter 9 | Fake It 'Till You Make It

I walked toward a table in the back part of the bar and proceeded to introduce myself. These patrons were employees of a new company called ESPN. I had never heard of it, but they proceeded to discuss their roles as producers on this sports network. All of them seemed very engaging and excited to be a part of a fresh platform. They were in town for the time trials and the Indy 500, they asked me what my other career path was, outside of waitressing.

"I am a writer," I replied. To this day, I can still remember how smoothly and quickly those words rolled off my tongue. The group invited me to join them at the correspondence booth the next day at the track, an invitation I could not refuse.

Arriving the next morning, an administrator asked me, "Who do you represent"?

I confidently replied, "Cosmopolitan Magazine." Once given a press badge, we jumped into a cart that proceeded to run in and out of all the pit areas. I sat next to the driver, with my press badge blowing in the wind. That day, I interviewed Kevin Cogan, Danny Sullivan and other drivers- each one asking when the article would be published. (Now that answer was a little tricky!)

In this whirlwind of pretend, I was invited to the suite of an NFL team owner for the 500 race, where I listened to Jim Nabors play piano and had dinner with Huey Lewis & the news. I introduced myself as a writer with Cosmopolitan, in fact it was repeated so often that day that a small part of me began to believe it.

Soon, it was back to normal life. I quickly realized that writing a book at night and working part time would not be financially-viable for my family. A friend of a friend approached me one day and stated that they thought I'd be perfect for car sales. I knew absolutely nothing about cars and really didn't care to, but there was one major perk: I got to use a vehicle *for free* while employed. With the need of a car, money, and stability, I walked into a dealership and applied. Within an hour, I walked out hired and began what would become a lifelong career in the automotive industry. It is an incredible industry of opportunity for those that are comfortable with failure. With my personality, failure didn't frighten me at all. I was an achiever and felt more than confident I could be successful.

Stories from the Road: Number 9

SOME PEOPLE JUST DON'T WANT TO LISTEN

As my business continued to grow, I needed to add an account rep. My preference was someone I had worked with before, and that they had working knowledge of what our team was set to accomplish. I selected a young and moldable person who appeared very hungry to succeed. He was with me for approximately two months when I received a frantic call from his wife.

"He's in the hospital with internal bleeding!" she shouted through the receiver.

I was so worried and very surprised that this was happening to someone so young. I immediately called the clients he was scheduled to visit, and they were begrudgingly understanding. The next 24 hours flew by as I waited to get a progress report on his health, but a report never came.

Little did I know, my account rep was never admitted into the hospital. During my time of worry, he and his wife were out purchasing computers and appliances, spending in excess of $10,000.00 on my company American Express card.

He disappeared, and I was stuck with the bill.

I thought I would never re-encounter this person, but several months later he resurfaced at a dealership. I immediately reached out to the owner to warn him.

"People in glass houses shouldn't throw the first stone," he said.

Obviously, my rogue ex-employee had shared a completely different version of the story, one that painted me as the bad guy!

I later learned that two weeks into his employment, my old account rep stole two cars from that dealership. Upon hearing the news, I called the store back. The receptionist answered and asked who was calling.

I said, "The woman in the glass house."

The owner never picked up my call.

Chapter 10 | My "AH-HA" Moment

On my first day in car sales, the sales manager told me to go outside and walk around the inventory. He further instructed that I should tell myself what I liked about the product. I could not help but think this was an odd example of leadership. *In fact*, I thought, *if this is training, we are in trouble.*

I proceeded to follow those that appeared most successful and learned to emulate their work process. It was a struggle that seemed so stupid. If any of us had solid skill training and management support, we would have really succeeded. I could clearly see there was a strong reason why most people failed in car sales.

I found myself drawn into a world where there was far too much down time and drifting. I knew that I had to do the opposite of what I saw most sales people doing.

One year into my automotive career, my general sales manager walked up to me and said that I was going to a training class the next day.

"Why me?" I responded, as if training was a form of punishment.

The class was in Cincinnati. I left later than I had planned and, on top of that, was stopped for speeding in my company car. By the time that I had finally managed to walk into the training room, the only seat open was right in the very front. People are always afraid of sitting front and center because, just like in school, those are the folks that always get picked on by the instructor.

As I took my seat, the facilitator asked me a question, "Did you work yesterday?"

"Yes, 12 hours," Okay, I was at the dealership for 12 hours but probably only worked for 2. He didn't need to know that, though.

"Did you ask for any referrals yesterday?" He challenged me.

In the automotive world, it is customary for sales people to ask customers for a referral *after* they sell a car in attempt to gain more customers. "No, I didn't sell anyone," I replied.

Now, for me, my response changed my life. I sat there thinking throughout the rest of the workshop; why in the world did I relate referrals with having sold a car? Why did I need to sell someone before I could prospect?

I drove back into work the next day and called everyone I had met in my first year at the dealership. I did nothing more than ask them all for referrals. As a direct result, I doubled my sold units and gross profit. Immediately.

The retail auto industry is a small world. Other people were asking me, "What happened? What had changed?"

I told them about the workshop and the contact information for the company that ran the workshop. I thought everyone should learn what I learned that day.

A few weeks later, these same individuals informed me that they had reached out to this company, but no one ever called them back.

Sitting in my office on a cold and rainy night, I decided that I would write a letter to the owner of this training company. I introduced myself and cut right to the chase; I told him that if he wanted things run right in his company, then he should hire me.

That owner called me as soon as he read the letter.

He flew in the next day and I was hired as his newest training consultant.

Stories from the Road: Number 10

JIM, THE MEDIOCRE ONE

While in Kansas City conducting a workshop for a local dealer group, I had a verbally loud nay-sayer in my training group. At nearly every turn of my training, he'd yell out why the process wouldn't work in their store. As this went on throughout the morning, I finally had to call him out.

"Listen, Jim, just because you have decided to carve out a mediocre life for yourself, don't try to bring the rest of us down with you!"

From that point on, he was silent.

Chapter 11 | The Breadwinner

I quickly learned how to be the top salesperson in my company. This afforded me an opportunity to better balance my work and home life. My children were little and beautiful. I could not help but feel a pang of guilt when I looked at them being raised by a single mother, however I do believe in my heart that one strong parent can make a difference- the love in our home, never suffered.

My son and daughter were the dearest of friends and played with each other day in and day out. It was the simple times of Big Bird dolls, building blocks and Thunder Cats. This new level of income was the first time, as an adult, that I wasn't consumed, in part, by financial worry. It was so refreshing.

As I grew stronger in my position, clients began asking for me to be their "on-site facilitator". In other words, I would be the person tasked to implement and conduct training. As with everything in my life, I immediately thought, *why not*!

I packed up my kids, rented a home in Glendale, Illinois and enrolled my children in school. They were 3 and 5, and the change was lot for young children. I remember my daughter crying each morning when I left her for daycare. It broke my heart. I could not stand to see her beautiful little face so sad, however it helped when I returned later to see her smiling again.

Life in Illinois was bringing new friendships and an increased professional confidence. I bought a brand-new Honda Accord, was making a strong income, and attempted to make a difference each day in the lives of my clients and my children. The company I was working for was growing, and a new avenue for training had recently opened-up. The Automotive Satellite Training Network, or ASTN- think of it as an automotive cable show. We had several programs constantly running. The training segments would range from customer retention, to developing client opportunities. One of my programs was called "Cool Under Fire". (Now, who thought of that title? Oh, yes, that was me!)

It gets better. Some of these shows were live.

One program that I convinced the producers to run was a life talk show with eight of our industry's most successful female car salespeople. I did not have the opportunity to speak with the guests prior to the show, so I sat next my panel and jumped right into the questions.

My first guest was a very attractive, confident woman, whom I hoped our viewers could relate to. As the show got started, I began the interview by asking her how she got involved in the automotive industry and what her secrets to success were. She went on to describe that she would flirt or sleep with some of the sales managers. Imagine my face. I was enraged, embarrassed. There I was, trying to promote professionalism and fight for women to have a place at the proverbial table... and this was our representation.

Stories from the Road: Number 11

A SEAT AT THE TABLE

I picked up a client in LA who owned one of the largest dealerships in the world. I appreciated working for a client who was incredibly successful, yet still sought my opinion for how they might improve. He was an old-school dealer, and the sales floor was completely comprised of men. Women did not yet have a seat at the table under this particular roof.

One day, the dealer invited me to join their sales meeting. As I entered the room, the men around the table looked as if they had seen a ghost. I laughed to myself, they had never seen a woman in this room before.

The dealer read their faces and justified his decision, "She is the only woman in business I can trust to tell me what I need to hear."

I took the compliment. My outspokenness had earned me a seat at the table.

Chapter 12 | Our Changing Home Life

Finding a work-life balance in a travelling consultant position was challenging. I loved my job. I was excellent at it, but at a high cost. I missed out on many of my children's life moments. Being so determined to provide my family with a level of financial comfort that I never had growing up, I chose to show up to work every day in different states, and sometimes even different countries.

The owner of this company had the same drive, passion and vision as me. We worked tirelessly to ensure the growth we felt the company was capable of, and through our shared passion and work, we fell in love. I cherished his ability to dream and his willingness to take chances. He lacked follow through, but I had plenty of that, so we made a good team.

You know what they say, "Behind every strong man, is a stronger woman."

Eventually, we married and merged our two families. My two children and his son from a previous marriage. We moved into a new home in Barrington, IL and I enrolled my kids in a Catholic school, sans the nuns (which was my preference).

Given my travel schedule, I knew I needed a full-time nanny to help look after my kids. The first attempt was a strict German woman, who reminded me of my grumpy grandmother. So, I swiftly removed her. There were several other attempts to secure the right person, but none lived up to my expectations. Just when I was about to give up, I got a call from my youngest sister, Jane. She and her husband were open to moving down from Wisconsin, and both needed jobs. It was agreed that my sister would take on the role of the nanny, and my brother in law would come to work with us in our consulting company. With them came my two young nieces and we suddenly grew to a house of nine. *The more the merrier*, I always thought!

With the blending of most families, there is usually some more difficult moments. These times came from my husband's son. I am sure, in part, it was overwhelming to go from the quiet life of a single child, to the home of chaos on the weekends. In fact, most of the times we were all together were filled with tension and frustration-atmospheres that dissipated when the child departed for his mother's house.

My husband also started showing a very odd level of competition with the kids. He played with them aggressively. It could be something as simple as a basketball game of horse with 8-year-olds, and he would play beyond competitively to show he could beat them. Very peculiar.

As a young man, my husband had told his father that one day he would make a million dollars. His father sharply replied, "What makes you think you are better than me?" With that father and son relationship, there was no wonder why he lacked a calm confidence.

As my sister got settled into her new role as our nanny, her husband began embracing his new role within our company. Travel was still a constant, but I felt great knowing my kids were in loving hands. We had grown our company from a team of 6 to 20. Our product was unique to the auto industry, so the limited competition made it easy to sell. Our business model offered popular workshops and onsite training sessions. Today, in fact, some of the auto industry's most recognized trainers had their start with our company.

-

It was at this time that United Airlines offered life time air passes. Pass holders would gain double the miles, fly first class anywhere and could "bump" anyone else out of their seat. The decision was made by my husband and I to invest in two passes, and myself being the consummate team player, decided to keep one pass under my husband's name, and the other as guest. This way, we could fly other employees and family members. The lifetime air passes were only available to purchase for approximately 2 weeks. Even at the cost of

1.75 million dollars, I believe the airlines realized this may not have been a great financial plan for them.

–

Our new families ran very smoothly together for a year. It was after this point that I noticed certain changes from my sister. Jane had always been super reliable, and now was displaying uncharacteristic behaviors, such as forgetting to pick up the kids on time and not answering the phone. When I confronted her about her behavior, she would simply smile and say, "Everything is fine."

I believed her.

We were friends with our neighbors, so much so that we even hired a woman that lived down the street to work at our office. All the kids in the area would play at the park behind our house; ride their go-karts in the cul-de-sac, play baseball and swim in our pool. It was fulfilling to see my children creating what would be lifelong friendships.

After a flurry of mysterious phone calls began trickling in late at night, we decided to change our phone number. Things grew quiet again.

At school, the kids were finding themselves, as well. My son had a school project to make a hand puppet from a sock. The instructions were very simple: Let the child make it. Later that week the puppets were on display at an open house. As I entered the room, it was filled with what looked like professionally made puppets... Except for my son's.

My son's green sock puppet had a black button for an eye that was crooked from the other.

"Really?" I said to the teacher. I now understood the "rules".

Shortly after, my daughter came to me with a contest on creating a yearbook cover. With my assistance, she created a cover that led her to win. Even though the taste of victory was nice, it really didn't bring the satisfaction we had hoped. It was at this point that my kids and I decided we'd much rather lose than to have someone else create their work.

These were wonderful years of innocence: the kids got in trouble for going to school with untucked shirts, I coached my daughter's cheerleading squad, and I was the scout leader for my son. However, the times I was away for work, the innocence seemed to unravel.

My sister became even more forgetful and I noticed signs of neglect for my children. We began receiving mysterious phone calls again, and like previously, when we answered, the call would disconnect. I never understood why, until one day when my neighbor, who we also employed, walked into my office with tears streaming down her face. I learned that afternoon that my sister had been having an affair with her husband.

I furiously confronted my sister. I wanted to punch her for committing such an act. Nothing I could do would fix this damage. My neighbor divorced her husband. My parents swooped in and helped pack up my sister, her husband and kids. "All of this is your fault," my parents said to me, "It's your lifestyle that caused this."

Another slap in the face.

Neither my mother or father would have the strength to truly look at what was happening to their youngest daughter. Her behavior wasn't her own. It was the silent killer of alcoholism that was taking over her life.

Luckily, through our arrangements over the past year and half, they saved every penny paid to my brother-in-law, so they were able to move back to Wisconsin and buy their first home.

Regardless of the events that unfolded, I loved my sister and her kids. My children grew so very close to their cousins and I had hoped they would remain so throughout their lives.

Stories from the Road: Number 12

YES, PEOPLE ARE REALLY LIKE THIS

Most car dealers are known for having rather ostentatious offices. I speak from experience, specifically, from an experience visiting a dealer in Denver, where I was given a picture that I will remember forever.

This owner had been married multiple times- not unusual for the characters I encountered on the road (though in his case, it was five times, so for anyone not named Larry King, this would still be considered a tad unusual).

Adorning the walls of his office, there were formal portraits of himself with each of his wives – past and present. This alone would be weird enough, but to make matters ever more bizarre, in each photo, the owner had altered his hair to match his partner's. In one photo, there he was with blonde hair next to his blonde-haired spouse; another with red hair next to a different red headed woman; and another of him with curly hair next to his curly-haired (presumably) ex-wife.

It's been said that if you can't say anything nice, don't say anything at all. I had a difficult time following this rule that evening in Denver.

Chapter 13 | Self-Destruction

I found out during this time that I had a tubal pregnancy. The affected tube needed to be removed, which meant I was left with only 1 damaged tube and zero chances of future pregnancies.

During the time I was in the hospital for this procedure, my husband was too busy at the office to stay with me, so I woke up alone.

The thought of no more children was fine. My children were perfect.

As our business continued to grow, my husband appeared to be less trust worthy of others and almost possessed a sense of paranoia. There were numerous opportunities that he could have taken in business, but his lack of trust always held him back.

The air pass we purchased from United provided us with the freedom to travel anywhere we wanted, at any time. For business this was excellent. For my husband, it was a disaster. He began to make stops at any cities with nearby casinos. This compulsion was something I had never witnessed before, and it was quite startling. It's as if the person is in a trance as they take over entire black jack tables, losing or winning at each hand. What started as innocent fun, was swiftly moving into a constant need for betting. As the stakes grew higher and the addiction stronger. It was common practice that we would go to a show in Las Vegas and when he'd leave to go to the restroom, simply never come back to his seat.

I finally got him to agree to go to therapy. It was a 6-week program, but after 2 days, he returned home. When I asked him, what could possibly be a sane reason for not completing this process, he said "I've got it all figured out."

With gambling comes emotional highs and lows. The anger and disappointment that came along with his addiction made him impossible to be around. He became argumentative and mean. I will never forget walking into the kitchen of our 2-million-dollar home and witness him stacking all the cans on the counter and coming up with reasons why I simply didn't need to go to the grocery store. The reality is that he didn't admit how much money he was losing. Now, to make matters much worse, he began picking on my kids. It was as if they were an easy target and he took whatever chance he could to make them frustrated or angry. After one particularly awful scene between he and the kids, I overheard them saying that once they graduated from high school, they would never want to come back home again. I was desperate to fix this mess that was consuming all of us.

It was in the middle of all of this that my doctor gave me rather starting news.

"You are pregnant."

I looked at him with shock, "You said that was impossible."

He replied, "Well, miracles do happen."

I walked away that day beyond ecstatic that I would be given the gift of life again.

I wondered if my husband would be able to find his balance again as a result of this news. Sadly, he did not. He was clearly too entrenched in his disease to find his way out. So, my best recourse was to book him with clients out of town as much as possible. This way, I could keep my kids calm and happy as they deserved to be.

Arguably, the best part about being pregnant is that you can eat for two and nobody will question you. (or at least that was the way it was back then). What's the worst part? The clothing, high collars, big bow ties, blue jean jumpers. I remember, as I approached the later months of pregnancy, I went back to the maternity store to find a larger size. The salesperson literally said, the next size up is "tent". Ouch.

To my daughter's dismay, her new baby sibling was going to be a boy. I wised up and had an epidural. What a difference that made! I felt no pain. The tough part was when the nurse said it was time to push. My legs felt like jelly, so I just asked if they could suck him out. My third baby was so beautiful. He held my hand at first breath in the world, and he has been the bright shining light for me, always.

The next day we arrived home, and my older children were so excited to meet their new sibling. My husband immediately demanded that they go outside and clean the van. As if the van was more important than this special life moment. I looked at him, knowing exactly what lied ahead. "Not now," I said pleading with my eyes. But he overruled me.

After that, he demanded they crushed cans. The list of chores grew, and as I watched him, I swore he'd be gone... soon. I had never met a person who lacked empathy the way that he did.

After a few months I decided to seek out a divorce attorney. While reading People magazine, I noticed the cover was dedicated to a divorce attorney from Chicago. I called immediately and set up a meeting. I assumed that if you were on the cover of People, you'd have to be a pretty good attorney, right? Well, I hired him immediately, and shortly thereafter, my husband was served and physically removed from our home.

As I gathered his belongings to send with him, I recalled something he used to constantly say to me when I would come home with new clothing or shoes. "You only have one pair of feet, why do need to buy more shoes?" So, I felt it was only fitting to provide him with only one piece of primary clothing.

"Where are my other clothes?" he yelled in frustration.

"You only have one pair of feet," I replied, "Why would you need more?"

The rest was donated to charity.

Stories from the Road: Number 13

DID THIS INTERVIEW REALLY HAPPEN?

As a consultant, I often help my clients hire new employees for their dealerships. At one dealership several years ago, I had an interview scheduled with a candidate for a sales position. I shook his hand and could not help but notice his eyes were bleeding.

Yes. Bleeding *actual* blood.

He apologized and said, "When I get nervous my eyes bleed."

Adding insult to injury, he also mentioned that he would have a belt on, but his wife was out of town and he couldn't find it himself. I guess he only had the one...

What do you think? Management material?

Chapter 14 | Peace at Last

It was the first time in years I felt at peace. The dark clouds that once rested above our lives finally parted. The kids and I were in utopia. I felt like I was in a scene from the movie Wizard of Oz, when the wicked witch was finally dead. We were all able to step out of the darkness, without looking over our shoulder every second, and be ourselves.

I was not concerned with my ex-husbands lack of presence, for as long as I could remember, I had run the house, the kids, and even most of our business – on my own.

Finally, I could do all the things without the stress of my ex-husband's toxicity. I learned more about women and our independence at this point in my life than any other before. One very crucial step to this independence, is women must learn how to make their own income. The games that people like to play with regards to submitting child support or alimony on time can be horrific, especially for a woman who is not financially independent. I knew that finalizing my divorce would not be easy. My husband obsessed over every penny-unless he was gambling.

My lawyer and I were scheduled to meet at my husband's lawyer's office. I thought I had the best in Chicago, until we walked into this office. Book shelves were stacked from the floor to the ceiling with self-written books and awards. My lawyer admired his adorned walls in awe, "Wow, you wrote all of these?"

I knew I was in trouble. A Cosmo Cover was nothing compared to the display before us.

I began kicking myself when I found out that my soon to be ex-husband was paying his attorney with miles from our United Air Pass-the one that I should have put my name on.

During our meeting, it was more than apparent that if I just let go of any real money, I could gain full custody of my son. There was no question here. I chose my son. Funny thing moving forward, any money received, was ultimately paid to me in miles from an air pass that I not only paid for, but truly should have already owned.

Is that *really* getting paid?

Following the finalization of the divorce, I hosted a huge FREEDOM PARTY. My ex-husband had a restraining order, so he could not come near us with his ridiculous behavior. Someone said they spotted him standing somewhere outside. I really don't know if he ever understood that all this loss was really his fault.

But life is about moving forward.

I was so happy to have my home in place.

As the business had truly grown with a lot of my efforts, I committed to trying to stay on with the company. I spent months attempting to keep the consulting team in place. This proved to be beyond challenging at times with questions, ridicule and sarcasm becoming a common thread.

One day, I'd had enough. I pulled my Jerry Maguire moment. I simply stood up in a meeting and said, "I am leaving, who's going with me?"

One associate stood up and joined me. Her name was Diane. We both left that office with no plan in place, got into my Jaguar and I drove away with a very large smile on my face.

Stories from the Road: Number 14

DON'T LET YOUR CLIENT BOOK YOUR HOTEL

There was one mistake that I made, which I never did again.

I let a client book my hotel.

As I pulled up to the entrance, a large sign displayed, "WELCOME PETS".

In the evenings, this hotel provided entertainment for its guests in the central atrium. One night I opened my door to head to dinner, and my attention was caught by a male strip show. Yes, in the atrium.

I thought to myself, "Where am I?"

As I made my way through the small crowd of women gathered to get a glance of a semi-naked man, I kept thinking, "I wonder if this owner stays here.

Chapter 15 | Becoming Independent

I soon found a small office space for rent in downtown Barrington where my kids could walk to easily after school. There I began to call all the contacts we had through our customer database, and I am proud to say that most were willing to come and work with my new team. I was told that my ex-husband phoned these same clients and complained that they were not being loyal to him.

Most simply responded, "Joni has been the one doing the work."

Now the tough part was building a strong team that could compete. We were in the auto industry, and this can be a very challenging platform. *Especially* for women.

For the first time, in a long time, I had a sense of ease. The stress and worry of money was there, but I didn't have anyone giving me grief. It's a wonderful gift to live in the moment. I was single, and I had a great circle of friends.

Among that circle of friends was my sister, Jackie. She was married and had a daughter. Although we did not live in the same state, no distance would break up our lifetime of friendship. My oldest sister Jean was re-married and living nearby in Milwaukee, while my sister Jane was trying her best to find her way back in Wisconsin.

-

This was the time of the Chicago Bulls' dynasty. My friends and I often took a limo downtown to the city and we'd go a game, then head to a bar that was frequented by many of the players. We'd dance the night away with NBA players, celebrating a successful season and the ease that came along with my new life.

One evening, I was approached by a player who demanded, "You need to come with me."

"No, thank you," I responded. Given the look on his face, I assume that this was not a response he was used to receiving. A sort of tantrum ensued, to the point where another player had to come to my rescue. I was thankful for his kindness after such an aggressive encounter with his team mate. I received flowers the next day at my office with a note of apology.

One night, as we were getting back into the limo, there was a homeless woman standing nearby. Her shoes were very old and torn. I asked her what her shoe size was, and it was the same as mine. I took off my new blue pumps and gave them to her. She smiled so big.

I happily walked back to my car barefoot. (See?! We *do* need more than one pair of shoes!)

One of my clients had played college basketball with a now powerful NBA star. I was invited to dinner that night and I must say, it was quite an evening. This individual kept talking about how a woman's place is behind a man. How a woman needs to know her place.

The entire table was silent and kept looking up at me to respond.

I simply waited for him to finish and then I had to state, "I had no idea what a fool you are."

Okay, so it wasn't the smoothest start to a dinner conversation.

As the evening moved on, I believe that he came to appreciate my strength. I just know one thing.

Take your stand my friend.

-

In a generous gesture, my sister and I were given a first-class trip to Europe. We would be gone 10 days, with the first stop in Athens. Upon arrival, our limo driver, Cosmo met us. He said, "Welcome to Athens, here we party all night and sleep all day."

I said, "Cosmo, I am finally home."

Fun.

That's all I can say.

I had my children at home securely cared for with my sister Jean, which allowed Jackie and I the ability to experience new parts of this world that should not be missed.

From Athens we moved on to Mykonos; Paris and then London.

In Mykonos we stayed at a breathtaking villa on the water's edge. They hosted a cocktail reception our first evening. As I walked down the double wide white marble staircase, I could not help but feel a little elegant. That was until I accidentally walked into the endless pool.

As the others looked at me, I couldn't help but hear the words they were thinking, *stupid American*.

In Paris, I dragged my sister in search for an American hamburger. When we finally found the spot, there was a man that kept staring at my sister. He was more than infatuated. When he came to sit near us, I asked him what he did for a living. He replied, "I carve the meats." I kept reminding my sister for years that she could have ended up with a balding, butcher from Paris!

In London we were able to be with a very dear friend of mine. We drank pints in pubs and regaled the life of a Brit. It is only through fate that Jackie and he would marry years later, and he would become a true family member.

Stories from the Road: Number 15

FIRING CLIENTS 101

I sat in a morning manager meeting to learn about a newly signed client and their daily work procedures. As the owner led this group he began to rant about the shitty customers with bad credit and dropping discriminatory comments. As his rants grew stronger, I stood up and began packing my briefcase.

"Where do you think you are going?" he snapped.

I stood up tall, looked him in the eyes and said, "I can't and won't work for someone like you. The customers you are describing with distaste are your customer base. Be thankful they don't know who you really are."

As I walked out the door, the room was completely silent. I know most of the managers at this meeting wished they could have left with me.

Just remember, always step up for what you believe in.

There was a great client opportunity in the Chicago area for a high-end product group and I arranged a presentation with the owner. When the day arrived, I was there early and prepared. As the owner asked me to join him in his office, he kept the door open and would constantly wave people inside. One by one he'd berate each employee, swearing and belittling them.

Approximately 30 minutes into my visit, I stood up and gathered my briefcase. I told him, this working relationship would not work out for my company.

Taken aback he said, "You know you are missing out on a big opportunity."

I smiled and said, "I am happy to not have you as a client."

Chapter 16 | The Teenage Years

Back at home, the kids were growing. I tried hard to stay involved in my children's everyday lives, but I was still traveling consistently for work, which made this difficult. Even when my older kids were able to take care of their younger brother, I always hired someone to keep 100% focus on him. It was a time of change and adulthood seemed to loom so close by.

I signed up as the Art Mom for my youngest son when he was in first grade. I overheard my son mention to his friends, "My mom doesn't really know art." And he was right. Our home didn't have any art on the walls. About a year after the divorce, I went to my kids and gave a clear choice. We could either stay in the 2-million-dollar home or move and go to college and vacations. Unanimously we voted sell! Conveniently, a woman approached me, interested in buying our pre-divorce home. So, we swapped. I got her house with the Japanese warrior wallpaper, and arched smoky brown mirrors, and she took over my rather new home. It was not a home of my choice, but one that would fit our family. I finished the basement, and this became my oldest son's space. We had 4 bathrooms, instead of 9, and three acres to have the kids grow up in.

Sports became the main focus of my oldest son, playing basketball, football and baseball any chance, he could get. My daughter was a skilled softball player, and I knew if she would have stuck with it, she could have played at the college level. My youngest son was an amazing, smiley toddler, who I doted on. They were delightful, growing and enjoying all the great things in life. We were living in a peaceful home filled with respect and the then the teenage years hit!

When my oldest son turned 16, I leased a new Toyota SUV for him. One week into the ownership, the driver door was ripped off at a gas station. It seemed he left the door open and backed up hitting a pole. Months later while pulling into the driveway, he ran into our brick house and shifted the corner of the garage.

The kids could never seem to keep a house key in their possession, but like me, they are solution-driven people. They would choose to jump into a basement well and pry the window open. One morning, in the middle of a cold midwestern winter, I walked by the basement door and felt a cold breeze. I walked down the stairs to find a 4-foot snow drift in the middle of the floor. This was the first time my kids and I shoveled snow from the inside out.

The age difference between my oldest and youngest son is 13 years. I overheard my youngest son on a playground once say to his friends that his brother drinks beer. They looked at him in disbelief and said, "How old is he?"

My oldest son was always extremely social. Even when he was a child, adults always seemed to gravitate towards him. In his teenage years, he was the "man of the house", although the house may have been mistaken as a hotel at times. One day I pulled up to our home and the double-sided driveway was filled with cars. I parked on the side of the road, and as I approached the house, I heard music blaring. In the backyard, the pool was filled with young adults, and the boys were cooking up a storm on the grill. I thought for a while that I had walked into Club Med. I must say though, unlike most parents, *it actually* made me happy. I loved the fact that my son felt so happy to be at home.

We hosted chaperoned New Year's Eve Parties, where we had each parent sign a waiver, and collected keys upon entry. Over the years, I took my oldest son and daughter on their own spring break trips. My son and his friends made the most of the relaxed drinking age by partying nearly every second of the day. I remember walking into Senior Frogs one night and saw my son dancing on the bar, so I decided I would take my leave. The next morning, I received a call from the Marriott front desk asking that I remove my son's friend from the entry way planter.

Later, as I was making my daily rounds and counting bodies, I knocked on the hotel room door to my son's room. He answered the door with a pierced ear and a tattoo on his arm. My mind wandered back to a conversation we had in his earlier high school years, when he asked me if he could have a pierced ear. I told him yes, only if he had straight A's for an entire semester.

That didn't happen.

"They are fake mom," he said with a smile.

Thank God.

The next afternoon, I rented a large boat for our group. There was a clear moment when we all looked around at each other, and the scenery, making mental notes of how lucky we all were.

His senior year in high school, he had to select a person they most admired in their life.

He picked me.

I cried when he chose me. It was a validation that I was doing something right. College was swiftly approaching, and I was excited when he decided to go to a local private school, where he could play football. When we visited the university, his excitement revolved around the "awesome" new cafeteria and football field. At least he had his priorities in line...

The college had students fill out a background form to help pair roommates. My son attempted to use reverse psychology by describing himself as "extremely fastidious" in hopes that he would be paired with someone who would keep the room clean. During move-in day, it was very clear that there were some large fundamental differences between these two young men: As my son hung up his Budweiser poster, his roommate put up a crucifix. I had sneaking suspicion the pairing might not work- and it didn't. My son's replacement roommate was just like him. His name was Tim, and they played football together and enjoyed the finer things in life together, like a great cafeteria. Years later, they are still dear friends and that warms my heart.

In the fall, I had huge signs made up to cheer my son on at his football games. We had a fan section that most kids would have been mortified by, but my son loved the attention. Because of his leadership skills, he was selected as a team captain and accountable to recruit new players each year. This was a difficult feat when the school's football record was a mere 2 collective wins over 4 seasons! I was very proud that he never quit. I can still recall the award banquets. The coaches made sure to steer clear of the win-loss columns and focus, instead, on some of the big plays that the boys carried out.

My daughter is so much like her older brother, but in a quiet way. Kate doesn't need to be the center of attention, while Ryan craved it. In hindsight, I don't think it was always easy for her, having such an outgoing older brother. Her comical and vivacious side could, at times, get swallowed up by the louder presence of her brother.

At the age of 13, my daughter met the man she would later marry. I picked her up one day after school and he was rollerblading around their school parking lot. She gushed about how cute he was. He had a pony tail and was not Catholic. My initial thoughts were this boy could be trouble. But I was so very wrong. He has grown up to be one of the most sincere and endearing individuals I have ever known. Being raised Catholic would have an everlasting feeling of conflict. I resented so many of the practices growing up, yet as an adult somehow clung back to these as if they brought comfort or familiarity.

On my daughter's spring break trip, she and her girlfriends shared a large room together, where they would chat constantly over cigarettes. One day I walked into their room for a "body count", and I could barely see through the clouds of smoke. These women were seriously planning their lives and enjoying the new freedom before them. I could listen forever to their dreams of heading to college and the changes they wanted to bring to this world.

As I write these words, I must say that my baby girl is one of the most real people I know. In these high school years, she didn't worry about fitting in. She spoke the words that were true for her. As a result, this didn't make things always as easy as they could have been, but it made her happy. As her senior year was drawing to an end, she set her sights on going out of state for college. I believe her need for independence was strong that helped her chose the University of Montana, Missoula. I was happy to know that her boyfriend and several other classmates had also selected this school. That part of our country is breathtaking; however, it's just so far from Chicago.

Her first application attempt to Missoula was followed by a letter of rejection. After receiving this letter, she flopped on the couch, crying. The image in her head of what her college experience would look like was taken away from her in that moment. She felt her life was over, even before it was started.

"No way." I told her.

We immediately drafted a response letter to the university which stated the other individuals we knew were accepted with lower ACT scores and GPA's, and we demanded they relook at her application.

The rejection was reversed.

I believe this taught her an invaluable life lesson: Always flight for what you want and never take the first No. (If you are anything like me, you won't even take the first 6!)

When the time came for my daughter to head to school, I had a really hard time letting her go. She had provided a certain calm for me ever since she entered my life. Anytime I look into her beautiful, sensitive green eyes, I can breathe a little better. I wanted to put crime scene tape across her bedroom door to keep everyone from entering. I always marvel when I hear parents so excited about their children going away to college. For me, a piece of myself left with her and I missed her terribly.

With two children away at school, my life began winding down. My youngest son was 8, and I think he probably felt excited to have the full attention at home. When I was away for work, I know he really missed me, and I felt guilty about leaving him.

I tried to keep him busy by enrolling him in baseball, soccer, and even Second City, but, while I am a great cheerleader, I wasn't exactly the best coach when it came to sports. I didn't have the skill set to show him how to excel at simple tasks like hitting and catching. I remember being at one of his little league games where he played rather poorly. I overheard a parent say, "That boy needs a father." I wanted to turn around and slap them.

I was just thankful that my son could not hear those mean words.

Stories from the Road: Number 16

DON'T GET KICKED OFF A FLIGHT IN THE MOUNTAINS

I will never forget Big Sky Airlines. They are no longer in business, and, in hindsight, I can understand why. My daughter had decided to go to college at the University of Montana in Missoula, so I was more than delighted to sign a new client in Billings.

A drive between these two cities would take hours and the mountains are vast and beautiful. Therefore, when my work would conclude in Billings, I would take a flight to Missoula. I always booked nonstop flights, however, they were never actually nonstops. It was quite the norm for the pilot to get on the speaker and say, "Folks were going to make a quick stop in Helena."

One evening, we flew into a heavy snowfall. Suddenly, the pilot announced that, due to the snow, we would not make it over the mountains unless we lightened our load. Once we touched down on this tiny, unsuspecting runway, the pilot walked down the center of our small plane and randomly selected a passenger to exit. I kept my head down during the selection process to avoid being picked.

As the pilot started the engines back up, I could not help but feel bad for the three people we abandoned. Looking out my small window, the snow swirled around their forlorn faces as the plane headed back down the runway into darkness.

Chapter 17 | A New Chapter

Have you ever seen the movie, South Pacific? Do you remember the song "Some Enchanted Evening"? The song goes like this: *Some enchanted evening, you may see a stranger, across a crowded room.* It is from a movie made in 1958. Yes, before I was born, but I have watched it many times, and that film still stays with me.

That "Some Enchanted Evening" song best describes the way I met my husband.

He is tall and strikingly good looking.

My friends and I stopped one evening at a nearby club. I saw him across the room and asked the bartender what he was drinking. I brought a drink to him, told him he was beautiful, gave him a kiss and left with my friends.

It's always good to make an impression.

The best thing is that he is intelligent, kind and so very loyal. It just feels so rare that we meet people who can lay action to words. People who can show through demonstration what they believe in, and not just vocalize it.

Over the next few months we would see each other and have lunch. It was the perfect way to slowly move a relationship forward.

Two qualities I think a person needs to look for in a potential partner are: Do they have a strong relationship with their mother and father? And do they have a strong circle of friends? He had both.

-

As this new chapter in my live moved forward, my youngest sister was continuing to struggle more than ever with her addiction. She was issued a DUI when driving to work at 8 AM. Her drinking was out of control, and she was losing all balance in her life. To provide positive support I flew her to Chicago to spend some time with me. As I left one morning to drive my son to school, I gave her a big hug. Upon my return she was laying on the couch complaining she was super tired. I covered her with a blanket and a couple hours later went back to check on her. She was completely incoherent. I then glanced over and noticed what had been a full bottle of vodka earlier that morning was now empty. She must have consumed the entire bottle in the 10 minutes it took me to get John to school.

I shook her to try and wake her. Unsuccessful. I carried her to my vehicle and took off for the emergency room. At the emergency room they told me her blood-alcohol level was dangerously high. They put her in detox and I found a way to pay for her to be placed in a 30-day program. I was so relieved that I could have her just a few minutes away. I could not help but think about how our lives had come full circle. How I could still remember being that scared 5-year-old girl, crying on the front porch and pounding on the door for my mom to let me in. Now, all I wanted was my baby sister to recover. To be whole.

After 30 days in rehab, my sister's husband and children picked her up and brought her home. She seemed clear and determined to start over. She made it known that she understood what it would take to be healthy and stay on a path of sobriety. But her ability to overcome this disease was cut short. She began drinking again daily and her behavior went back to being erratic. In this time when she needed her husband the most, he filed for divorce from her. It just was too much for him. This disease was stronger than anybody could fathom. My sister's experience with AA was disastrous. Her sponsor broke the cardinal rule and began sleeping with her, despite himself being married.

For Christmas, to bring the family together, I gifted everyone a box filled with sand, sunscreen, and a beach ball. On the gift was a note that said I had rented 3 homes on a lake outside Chicago for a week that coming summer. I anticipated a fun family filled week, but my sisters were either living in another state, struggling with addiction, or living in a toxic relationship, so the only people there for the entire week were my parents and my children.

I will never forget my younger sister arriving with her new boyfriend, who was a bartender (Not exactly the best person for a recovering alcoholic to be dating). When I had a moment to talk with her about this, my mother was beside me, and I voiced my concerns about the toxicity of the relationship; and I wanted to make sure he knew that she was an alcoholic. My mother jumped in saying, "Well, I don't think she needs to tell everyone."

Once again, my mother always attempted to keep this false image on the surface. As if it was better to stuff down any feelings or actions that would not be deemed attractive.

On my way driving home from that week, I had a special voice mail. It was from my future husband. He stated, "If you aren't married, call me."

I phoned him back.

From that day moving forward, we never left each other's side.

A couple years later we were married in St. Thomas at the Ritz. It was breath taking. We said our vows in a gazebo along the beach.

He learned how to sail, and we went nearly every day.

It was an amazing time in our lives, and something we relive as often as possible.

Stories from the Road: Number 17

NADA

In the auto industry, there is an annual convention hosted by the National Automobile Dealers Association (NADA). Through the years it has been a popular and powerful platform for earning new business and strengthening current ones. All connected convention hotels run continual footage of the show for the entire 4 days.

In our convention booth area, we would host small brief training sessions. This not only attracted potential clients, but it was a great way to demonstrate our product.

One afternoon, a couple joined into the seating area. They chose the back row and proceeded to make out. It was hilarious. I certainly did not expect this type of display at our booth in a convention hall.

Later, I would find out that the dealer who was passionately kissing this woman was a married man, and that was not his wife. Short thinking on his part, this make out session was recorded and played in everyone's hotel rooms. Yikes, his wife was definitely not a happy person.

Back in the day, the NADA evening functions were formal occasions. I recall drinking a Miller Lite from a bottle in a formal evening gown and conversing with a group of women. Amidst our conversation, one of the ladies said, "Women do not drink beer out of a bottle."

"Real women do," I replied with a smile.

A couple nights later, as I attempted to "boogie down" on the dance floor, I saw the same group of women, only this time they all had a bottle of beer in hand. They raised and toasted to me with a smile.

Chapter 18 | Love and Loss

My sister continued to struggle with her addiction. On the day my father was at the hospital getting his knee replaced, I had taken my sister to the same hospital for detox. Her addiction held such a tight grip on her that she would pull her IVs out during the early evening; and put on her clothes; go to a bar and then go back to the hospital.

It was out of control.

One day, I received a phone call from my father. "Well, the worst thing has happened, your sister is dead."

I fell to the floor.

I loved her so very much and the immediate reality of my sister being put into the ground was frightening. There was nothing more final. Dead. I had spent years rescuing her, and then, suddenly, she was gone. A part of me felt such guilt that I resented her initial presence in my life. Another part of me felt such deep sadness as to how I would ever live with this type of loss.

But I wasn't the only one she left behind. Our family, my sisters, her three children who were 7, 11 and 12 years old, so very young and they were never going to be the same. I also found out later that she tried her reach her sponsor three separate times that evening. He didn't answer any of these and, within a few hours, she was dead.

The day after her death, we drove to Madison to help select her coffin prepare for her funeral. I had never been to a funeral home to shop for casket before. The setting reminded me of a car dealership with special lighting on certain models, and upgrades from her picture on candles to matchbooks etc. It was awful. I will never forget the look on my father's face. Actually, it wasn't his face. It was his eyes. They lost their light. Part of him was lost that day she died, and it would never be brought back.

My youngest sister and I loved Bruce Springsteen and we promised each other that when we died, we would have his music played at our funerals. Unfortunately, I was shot down by the Catholic church. I felt so bad, as I know my sister would've been enraged at the thought of her funeral being this painfully drab, formal and boring. Once again, my struggle with the Catholic church would continue.

A couple years later, my father, who was a driver that took elderly people to their doctor appointments, would leave my mother on a rather normal morning.

I used to kid him by saying, you're an elderly person.

This particular day my father gave my mom a kiss on her cheek and said he looked forward to having dinner that night (He loved to cook).

After he picked up Catherine, a 93-year-old woman heading to a doctor appointment, he screamed in pain. Knowing my dad so well, even in pain, he pulled the van over the side of the street to be safe and slumped over the steering wheel.

My father suffered a fatal brain aneurism. He died without any warning.

When I reflect on my father, this was the perfect way for him to die. He was always going to go out with a bang.

The real problem was with the shock this had on my mother. We can all sit back and try to debate would you rather have time to say good bye because of an illness; or just die – without warning. For my mother, she was in shock. My father had paid all the bills and balanced all the books. She had never even put gas into a car. Though it has been over ten years later at the time I'm writing this very book, my mother is still is in complete denial and shock. To make matters worse, she is now struggling with a brand-new dilemma: a battle with dementia.

It's a new living nightmare.

Chapter 19 | Acceptance

As I came to accept the loss of my sister and father, I was able to allow myself to live a more normal life. My husband became the coach of my youngest son's baseball game for several years. This gave my son the skill training that I could not provide; and the support to advance as he could potentially do. Let's face it. He finally had a father figure that he deserved.

Unlike myself and his older siblings, I enrolled my son in public schools. I wanted him to have the opportunity to think for himself and not have decisions made for him. Thanks to the influence of his public schools, he is an independent thinker in so many ways. For example, he has been a steadfast vegetarian since 6th grade. My baby boy has grown up to be a political activist; gifted writer; old soul and a graduate from Marquette University. I feel John is comfortable going against the grain. Catholicism pushes followers to conform or get out. I love John's independent views.

Proudly, my older children have each earned two master's degrees; and married the loves of their lives.

I must say that giving away my oldest son to be married was a tough step. This is probably true for most mothers. It was just so hard to walk away from the continuity of knowing that he had always be there first and foremost. Also, the reality is that I had always been accountable for his life, no one else; and then it was time to pass this on to another person. While it was easy to share in this joy of their marriage; it was also at times a mix of bittersweet emotions.

With my daughter's wedding I felt more of a shared joy that day. She and I were together early in the morning, walking over for coffee on what looked like a rainy day ahead (it was on outdoor wedding) and were in a centric place. Perhaps it's just the difference between men and women. A daughter and mother's relationship are simply platformed on more common ground. Her wedding day turned sunny and they were married along a beautiful river. Just the perfect venue.

You see this destination matched the two of them as they were always a couple that was more nature focused. I think back on their Montana college days where they filled hours in the rivers fly fishing; and climbing The M.

Within my son's first year of marriage, I turned 50; and became a grandmother. My first grandchild was a beautiful baby boy, Jackson. All of it amazing; however fast!

My grandson looks just like my oldest son, only Italian. His breathtaking beautiful face took all of us aback by his bright and curious expressions.

Within another year, we all welcomed another grandson, Cameron. This miracle looking more like my daughter with big almond eyes that can melt your heart the moment he engages with you.

The families were growing, and I was so very proud to see that my oldest son was becoming exactly the type of father he always wished he could have. He and his wife were a unified team and their relationship balance could be felt from afar. Three years later, we welcomed their third son, William. He is simply beautiful. Now, I am thinking of that old tv show, "My Three Sons." Remember, Fred MacMurray? It was a popular show from the 1960s where it represented an openly caring father of three sons. Yes, that is what my son wanted, although I believe he would picture himself more along the lines of Clark from "The Griswolds".

My daughter welcomed her first child several years after their wedding- a stunning baby girl named Molly. Her eyes are like crystals and she possesses a smile that never ends. She enters the room with full force and determination, and I do not doubt for one moment that she will take over this world in some capacity.

As our home became quieter with all the children gone, we settled more into our lives. Although in Illinois, we keep our swimming pool heated to 92 degrees through the first week of November. Our pool is basically a hot tub. As the leaves begin to fall from the trees and the cold winds blow, you can see a steady stream of heat rising from the water. We keep stand up heaters strategically scattered around the patio to ensure we can watch movies or football games while floating. Let's face it, though, November is when the snow begins to fall, so it's time to cover up the pool and dream of next April.

With the years that have swiftly flown by, I have continued to successfully build a strong group of team members within my own company. My husband is the cornerstone and lends his wisdom far beyond that of a father or husband. My focus remains the same: To take over the world and make it better. Whatever part of the world that is.

I have been fortunate to also expand my reach outside the auto industry, to consult within the RV industry, jewelry industry, NASCAR resorts and 5-star resorts. I can't help but laugh when I think about being hired to help an amusement park improve its operations, and the first changes that comes to mind is adding more balloons. Now, that's a smart plan!

Chapter 20 | March 7th, 2017

On March 7th, 2017, I flew into Phoenix with the intention of working two days for a long-standing client. That day was routine. Once I landed, their driver picked me up and whisked me directly to their dealership. I focused on reinforcing the performance standards for all departments and kept accountability in place. I am very proud of this account because, with my help, they have more than doubled their business and profitability.

On my way home after work, I remember thinking how smoothly life was going. In fact, for one moment I took a deep breath and smiled that business and family were both doing so well.

Just as I pulled to a stop on the two-lane highway to wait for traffic and make my left turn, I took that breath and within seconds I was nearly dead.

BAM! I was hit from behind by a vehicle driving 60 miles per hour. My seat broke from the impact.

BAM! I was hit from the front by another car driving 60 miles per hour.

As a direct result, the lap portion of the seat belt turned and eviscerated me. In other words, it turned and became a large knife that cut through my mid-section. Fire broke out and I faded out of consciousness with the sounds of sirens whirling around me. I was told later that initially at the scene they pronounced me dead.

I wasn't.

I had approximately two minutes before death could become a reality. Just think, those two minutes were the difference between seeing my children, my husband, my grandchildren, my sisters and my friends again. Luckily, one of the passengers in a nearby vehicle called 911 for an emergency helicopter to swoop in and take me to the nearest hospital.

The next 48 hours were touch and go. One of my nieces that lived nearby was the first to arrive. My husband, daughter and middle sister were there within 24 hours, and I was told that my daughter went into a loud fit. She screamed and shouted that "this was wrong" and that "I was too loving and caring and did not deserve this." Awe, my baby girl.

My sons arrived the following day.

I remember nothing. From what I have been told, I broke two vertebrae, my collar bone, my shoulder, my arm, my leg, my hip. I had severe head trauma and lung damage. I lost part of my lower intestine, stomach, gallbladder.

You name it.

I was a mess.

I spent the first 60 days in the ICU.

My stomach area was hollow, and I had a tracheotomy. I remember drifting in and out of consciousness and thinking, "Where in the world am I? What happened?"

34 Surgeries later, I regained consciousness. My new reality was that I could not speak. Even though, in my mind, words were coming out of my mouth, everyone around me just stared as I strung together an arrangement of incomprehensible sounds.

Wow, I can't talk. My voice was my life. I had no idea how this could have happened to me.

I dreaded nights more than anything. Doctors were required to perform routine checkups that interrupted my sleep to ensure that my body's responses continued to progress. Despite how much of a traumatic blur everything was at the time, I'll never forget the gut-wrenching fear of falling asleep. I can only speak for myself, but I will say that when "present" for extended periods of time at a hospital's ICU, you're consciously aware of your own mortality. You'll always be afraid that the next time you fall asleep, you may never wake up again.

Once the swelling in my brain reduced, the doctors were more relieved.

With the help of an extremely strict speech pathologist, I began speaking again. Her simple entrance into my hospital room would fill me with dread. She demanded very painful vocal exercises that I just didn't want to face. Even though I really could not stand her toughness, I knew she was the best. Part of her job was also to determine when I could eat solid food again. Let me describe, this was a very powerful position.

Hunger. I had never been this hungry and I don't think I will ever forget that feeling.

I used to literally pull on the lab coat of a doctor or nurse and beg (in squeaky sounds) for any type of food. It had been months without anything.

Once my voice was coming back, I told an ICU nurse I would give her 1 million dollars for a Diet Coke.

The only food I could have after I came out of my month-long coma, was a communion wafer. With that in mind, I decided I would ask for the Chaplain a couple times a day. I can still see the look on the nurse's face when I would ask to see the Chaplain again. They probably thought I needed religious guidance, when I sincerely just wanted the wafer.

My poor niece was there constantly and would have to be the tough one to say no to my pleads for more ice chips. I was only allowed 5 ice chips a day. I was starving and in more pain than I am able to describe.

Finally, I improved enough to be able to breathe and swallow on my own. With this accomplishment, I could finally eat real food. My tough pathologist- with a very big heart- brought me home made mashed potatoes. My favorite.

Food never tasted so good.

Throughout all my months in the hospital my husband never left my side. Ever. He is 6 foot 5 and would attempt to sleep on a small chair night after night. I never really understood how much he loved me until this selfless display.

Nurses often regaled stories to me about how so many spouses "bail out" during a crisis like this. My husband was not that type of person.

I am *so* lucky.

This accident also shed light on one of my truest friendships. My very dear friend Carol from Chicago visited with me every few weeks. Spending so much money that I know she never planned on. Her commitment to our friendship was and is something truly remarkable.

All my children, and my sister, Jackie, sacrificed so much during these months to be there for me. Even my poor grandsons were dragged to sit and spend a week beside their broken grandmother. My granddaughter just looked at me with curiosity and wanted to run free.

It was all the love and support that people brought my way, that helped me survive. We all know that we die alone. I know one thing, I had so many people in my life that simply weren't going to let me die. I owe so many, so very much.

One day, I simply had enough of being in the hospital. When a nurse came in to take my vitals, I told her I was leaving. She responded, "How are you going to get out of here?"

I told her I was going to walk.

"You can't walk," she responded.

I looked at her in surprise.

I had no idea I was incapable of walking. Yet another challenge I would have to overcome.

I would lay in bed just listening to the wound vac inside me with tears running down my cheeks thinking, *how in the world did I get here?* I just wanted to go back in time.

On rare days, I had the strength and energy to go outside. My husband would ask for assistance, so I could be wheeled outside for a moment of sunshine. I looked like Steven Hawkins in my wheelchair. I was all bandaged and broken. I often hoped I would wake up and things would be back to normal.

The only bright spot- which, of course I had to find one- was that for the first time in my life, I didn't worry about money. I felt that weight off my shoulder. I could not think about selling, budgets and goals. I wasn't capable.

The tough part of that equation, though, is everything was left on my oldest son's shoulders. My husband had vowed to immediately quit his role and stay beside me. Now, my son was in charge. He had joined the company approximately one year ago and was tasked with trying to maneuver it all. Thank god, my son in law was there with him, and together I knew they would do the very best they could to make it work.

My hospital rooms were decorated from floor to ceiling with cards and photos. Anyone who walked into the room could feel the love and support. My Arizona client would have his therapist up once a week to massage my feet with hopes of building circulation.

And my hair, *oh* my hair. As I had to lay in bed for months, it became such a tangled mess they had to cut it all off. My signature long blonde hair. *Years* of growing were gone.

I felt so ugly.

Finally, after a few months in the hospital the plastic surgeon was brought in. He took skin grafts from my leg to try and build a new stomach area (Great, my legs now look like a checkerboard). The tiny fragments of glass were so embedded in my stomach area the wound vac was working overtime, and my surgeon told me that he had never seen internal organs so compressed.

Four months after the accident came the time to relearn how to walk. It started by becoming acquainted with a wheel chair. I had never used one before, so I was slow to adapt. I had moved to a rehab facility, and leaving my nurses was tough. Some of them were the most giving and loving people I have had the honor to meet.

Now, the rehab center was circular. The gym and dining area were located directly across from my room. It was probably about a 10-minute walk for a functioning adult. With my lack of skill in the wheel chair, it would take me approximately 45 minutes to get there. I think I was moving at the pace of snail. At the facility was an elderly man named Eddie. He was probably in his 80s and loved to regale on his life's experiences. Eddie was the type of man who wore a hat with fishing corks hanging down. One day, I decided, instead of going around to the gym, I would cut directly through the middle court yard area. Brilliant plan that It was, as I attempted to enter one of the outer door ways, I became stuck. Great, here I was with the door closing in and out on me. Suddenly, I heard a loud voice from behind me. It was Eddie. "Don't worry, Joni, I can save you!" Suddenly he wheeled over and pushed me through the door way.

I laughed and smiled and said thank you.

Eddie you do realize we are the combined age of approximately 140 years old!

He was a sweet man, and I hope he is well today.

My husband continued to help me heal, and swiftly became an expert at changing my wound dressing. My stomach area was and is a disaster. It looks like a wild animal attacked me. I guess a car can be a wild animal; or a failing seat.

The only word I can think of to describe my middle section of my body is gruesome.

That's it.

I believe my husband's great gift for caring goes back to his mother. They had a wonderful relationship. In the midst of my recovery, he received the word that his mother's kidneys were failing. She was 94 and did not want any type of treatment. He returned home to be beside her during her last days.

My poor husband.

With my husband away, my youngest son assumed the duty of coming to Arizona and staying beside me- that brings a smile to my face, even as I type this. We chilled out over pizza and ice cream; watching movies and finally breathing.

As my days in rehab grew and my progress improved, I convinced one of my doctors to remove the cast on my left leg. I had spent countless days learning how to walk with my right leg, but I wanted to be able to use both. I imagined the scene from Forrest Gump when he started to run, and his braces fell off. I thought, that will be me. I returned to the gym in my wheelchair and stood up. I started to take my first step, but instead of strength, I found a new weakness and fell right down. People in the gym could not help but giggle. I forgot that a broken leg, if not used for several months, atrophies. That just meant another big hurdle ahead.

On top of all of this, I had not showered in months. Even though the thought of a shower sounded great, part of me was so frightened to try and stand- I had an enormous fear of falling. I would rather have crawled into a shower than to try and stand.

But I did it.

I inched my way in and out of a chair. My body was slow, but my mind was back, and back strong. The rehab had very strict schedules and time tables. My release date was posted, and they did not want to waiver. This policy was soon to be broken as my husband's mother died and he had to be home for the funeral. I was taken in my wheelchair to see my plastic surgeon for one last time, and when whisked to the airport. As the plastic surgeon looked at his work, he taped on my right hip bone, which now sits approximately 4 inches too far to the right, and said "Gee, I hope you will be ok with that."

I said, "With what?"

Keep in mind, I have never looked at myself since all this happened. I didn't even realize that my belly button was gone, that I was left with two large flaps of skin, and a center bound of thin red flesh.

Awful.

So, I sat there at the Phoenix airport scared. Quiet. I felt like someone who had been kept in solitude and then set free. I was in awe of watching how people walked with ease. Something that I had taken for grated of in the past. I kept thinking how in the world did this happen to me.

As the wheel chair staff took me to the gate, I had to be transferred to another wheel chair that could place me in my seat. All the other passengers were staring at me. I felt like the "elephant man", and I just wanted to be normal again.

For the over 3-hour flight I never moved. Forget the bathroom.

I was heading back to Chicago.

What happened, was still all I could think of.

I was only going to be in Arizona for two nights.

Here I was in flight with 3 million dollars in hospital debt; the inability to walk; the loss of clients; personal physical body disembowelment. How could this have happened?

Chapter 21 | The New Normal

I was freed into the real world, and yet, I didn't feel like I was the real me. I arrived back home and literally was overcome with fear as to how I could even get through the front door.

My husband had set up our home to accommodate my new handicaps, and while so appreciated his efforts, it all just broke my heart. When I first sat in my new mobilizing chair, I started to realize that I would never be normal- that was taken away from me on March 7th. While others still marvel every day that I am able to walk, talk, eat and process foods, I still miss the *old* me more than words can describe.

We now sleep in the guest room off the kitchen because I can't walk upstairs. I have a Physical Therapist who comes to my home and holds me while I cry. I have moved to using a walker and face the daily challenge of walking in circles around the first floor of my home. My sister, Jackie, comes to my home every week to stay with me, my children are always there with me, and a very dear friend of mine has become my Wednesday night chef. These days I have spent most of my time just waiting for the freedom to put myself into bed and go to sleep.

I hate where my life is now. Hate it.

Our pool is open, and I can't go in.

I have open wounds, and, with well-water, I can't shower.

I have missed birthdays, graduations, so many life events.

In early November, I was sitting in bed and realized that I had an enormous number of lumps throughout my breasts. I slowly sat up (which was tough as I have zero stomach muscles) and cried. *Great, I survived all this to now have breast cancer.*

I took an immediate trip for a mammogram, which provided a happier diagnosis. While learning I was cancer free, another new reality set in: I have multiple blood clots that formed from the impact of the accident. The specialist calmly told me that the bad news is they will probably never go away.

Great, another new normal.

My first important task at home was to find a facility for Physical and Occupational Therapy. I loved my Physical Therapist, Nancy. She was funny and strict at the same time. I arrived to our first meeting her with a walker and left after a year later, walking (almost consistently) straight.

I remember one of the first days, I stood in front of the full mirror at Physical Therapy and told her, "You know, I use to be cool."

With a wink, she responded sarcastically, "I'd like to see a photo of *that*."

I needed that sense of humor. Laughing, though painful, was the best medicine for me. It is only because of people like Nancy that I was able to stay strong through the times I wanted to quit.

The first time I looked at my body I screamed.

I could not believe how deformed I was.

I also could not believe how foolish I was to ever think that I was exempt from this type of trauma. I was ignorant to think I would ever be able to be the way I once was.

This was my new normal. Something that happens to people all over the world, every day. I had to remind myself that tragedies are called tragedies for a reason- they strike those who don't deserve it.

Words cannot describe how unfair and wronged I continue feel by what happened that day. But I knew when I was fighting to recover in the hospital, as I know now, that people needed me to get back up.

I had built a successful life by being tenacious and never backing down. And you could be damn sure that I wasn't going to allow this freak accident to get in the way of who I was.

Against all expectations, I found the strength to work again. A couple days per week slowly became 4 days per week. I began traveling to visit clients and telling my story on keynote stages around the country.

I knew I could do it – I never lost faith.

STORIES FROM MY LIFE

I lawn bowled in a fishing village called Iluka in Australia; I jumped from a 4 seat sea plane into a row boat in the middle of the great barrier reef and spent hours snorkeling and scuba diving with no land insight; I rode a scooter bike in total darkness through the mountains of Mykonos; I flagged down a police car and convinced him to turn on his sirens to get my sister and I to a Rolling Stones concert on time; I sat front row at one of the last live performances of Moulin Rouge in Paris; I took a private water taxi in Venice, Italy and spent the evening at a breathtaking, floating casino and bar; I grabbed pieces of the Berlin wall while in Berlin; I crawled through the floors at the Hotel Du Louvre in Paris and changed the door tags on rooms which meant people were woken at wrong times or got their shoes shined when not requested; I led the opening of Class A Motor Coach Resorts – with no experience; I conducted workshops in Puerto Rico without knowing how to speak Spanish; I walked through the outback in Australia with barefoot guides & drank cold Toohey's beer in pubs with cows walking through; I privately sailed the beautiful waters in St. Thomas; I joined 12 pyramid water skiers throughout the lake of the Ozarks; I sat out all night in Finland and embraced the Midnight sun.

The experiences I have had are so unique and uncommon.

I embrace all the new adventures ahead.

Epilogue

So, why "Eat the Burrito"?

For as long as I can remember, I have never been a thin woman - That is, unless you count the time following March 7th when I was starved for a couple months. I have always loved Mexican food. My favorite local restaurant is Lily's, which is only a few minutes from my home in Northwest Chicagoland.

When you go into a restaurant and look at the menu, I always believe there are two types of "voices" who are saying two completely different words.

The "good side" says don't eat the sour cream; no margaritas.

The "bad side" says, go for it! You only live once. In fact, I have always thought how mad I would be if I really restricted what I wanted to eat, and then you died.

My first doctor stated to me that with the impact of the vehicle; the broken seat; and the seat belt turning into a knife, if I was a think woman, I would have been severed in half.

But, because I had "girth" (which is a polite way of saying pounds), I lived.

So, the moral of the story is what?

EAT THE BURRITO...
IT COULD SAVE YOUR LIFE!

Acknowledgements

I would like to acknowledge Dr. Nicholas Thiessen, who saved my life.

Thank you, as well, to the entire team of physicians, nurses and therapists and Chandler Regional Medical Center who helped me overcome the greatest challenge I have ever faced.

30487537R00094

Made in the USA
Lexington, KY
09 February 2019